THE STORY OF
One Hundred Symphonic Favorites

THE STORY OF
One Hundred
Symphonic
Favorites

By PAUL GRABBE

Grosset & Dunlap
PUBLISHERS
NEW YORK

To Gardner

To Gardner

CONTENTS

Contents

Contents

[ix]

Contents

[x]

Contents

Contents

On the Enjoyment of Music

A STORY, TOLD HALF IN JEST, is that the Shah of Persia, while on a state visit to Russia, was taken to the opera by the Tzar. When asked if he had enjoyed the performance, the visiting potentate is said to have expressed great pleasure—especially with that part of the music which came "before the man in the orchestra pit started waving his stick."

This amused the Russians immeasurably, making them feel very sophisticated and cosmopolitan. Yet, had they traveled to Persia, they would perhaps have evoked similar smiles. Lacking the necessary familiarity with Persian music, they, too, might have derived more pleasure from the tuning than from the playing. More than likely, they would have found the playing confusing and boring—for the enjoyment of any music is predicated on familiarity.

On the Enjoyment of Music

A music lover does not necessarily possess musical erudition. The majority would be incapable of analyzing a symphony or of defining the meaning of the word *canon* except as an instrument of war. All share one characteristic. They possess a "listening acquaintance" with the music they enjoy. This listening acquaintance means that they have heard a composition a sufficient number of times to have become familiar with its principal melodies and subdivisions. They can anticipate the music as it unfolds. They are prepared to enjoy it when it comes. When deeply moved they follow it tensely, almost breathlessly.

It is in this respect that music differs from, say, the movies. A movie is enjoyed fully when it is witnessed for the first time. Indeed, few movies contribute more—and the majority contribute less—enjoyment when viewed a second or a third time. Exactly the reverse is true with music. A musical composition, especially a complex composition such as a symphony, may not really be "heard" when one listens to it for the first time. Only through repeated hearings does the mass of sound gradually take shape, sort itself out, and assume a definite meaning.

The listener, then, is in a sense a participant in the music he hears. He cannot enjoy music by being merely a bystander, and he does not obtain his enjoyment for nothing. What he contributes is familiarity; and, through familiarity, he brings to the performance of a composition the attention required to follow it as it develops.

To the enjoyment of music the listener brings something else as well. He brings his likes and dislikes; also, his mood of the moment which predisposes him to hear this or that music, or perhaps not to hear music at all. He may, for example, be familiar with both Beethoven and Mozart, but may find neither of these composers—to him—as meaningful as Brahms. Yet, he may not always want to hear Brahms. He may be in the mood for Stravinsky's blatant and colorful *Petrouchka,* or crave the poetic eloquence of Smetana's *The Moldau,* or feel that nothing else will do but Debussy's elusive, sensitive *Nocturnes.*

With music as with food people's tastes differ and the appetite is selective. But who is to say what, at my stage of musical development, I must find exciting, or moving, or satisfying—and when?

Actually, there is no "must" in musical tastes and musical moods, no obligation to like music because it is Beethoven's, or Wagner's, or César Franck's; or because it is performed by some world famous musician. There is every reason, in fact, for liking some things and disliking others. In music as in love one is subject to passing enthusiasms, to unaccountable fleeting passions. In music, too, enduring attachments do not develop overnight. It is the titillating titbit which immediately affords the greatest pleasure, while the more solid type of musical fare does not yield itself completely on first acquaintance. Not that it is forbidding. It is merely unknown, and the unknown is seldom pleasurable. To be enjoyed, music must first be "contacted."

This matter of contacting music—of having a composition suddenly mean something beside a mass of bewildering sound—is dependent not only on the listener but also upon the performer. To be heard, music must necessarily be performed, and a good performance is as essential to the listener's enjoyment as is the familiarity with the music and the receptive mood which he himself contributes. Unfortunately, the inspired performance is rare. One may listen to a composition many times over, yet never find it more than mildly interesting until one day its meaning is revealed through a superlative performance. The listener then wonders whether this music is the same as that which he has heard so many times before. This question is not easily resolved.

Music, in its performance, especially music requiring the joint effort of many performers, is a complex undertaking. Even slight miscalculations in speed and volume, especially the former, may distort a composition, rendering it meaningless. Though the composer marks on his score all that he can, he cannot indicate his full intentions. At best he can only suggest. A great deal of leeway in interpretation always remains in the hands of the performer—the conductor in the case of symphonic music—and performers with a sure sense of what is right are scarce. There are not many first rate conductors in the world.

But even the outstanding conductor is not

necessarily infallible. He is not a machine; he does some things better than others; he may somehow fall just short of the ideal performance for reasons unaccountable.

In this respect recorded music has much to recommend it. Although it has not yet been perfected so it can match, even at best, the same performance in the concert hall, the record does "immobilize" the music. The superlative performance, once captured on a record, remains superlative. Seemingly, it may defy even the steady technical advance which characterizes record making. This is not hard to understand. What counts primarily in music is its meaning, dependent heavily upon interpretation. If this is masterly, even in spite of the availability of more recent versions, the older recording may remain the best for years.

Of such exceptional recordings there are many, but to find one's way to them is not always easy. There may be five or six, or even more different recordings of the same music in the various catalogues. To discover which of these recordings is the best may be, if not impossible, at least impracticable.

On the Enjoyment of Music

Because I have myself often experienced this perplexity, it occurred to me that this book could make a real contribution by providing a list of the best available recordings pertinent to this discussion. With this in mind—since my own knowledge with the field was limited—I turned for help to the Gramophone Shop in New York, an organization internationally known for its pioneering in the distribution of good recorded music. I turned to this organization chiefly because its monthly Record Supplement, giving a strictly non-commercial critical evaluation of all recent releases, had won my confidence through the three years during which I have been a subscriber to this service.

To Mr. George Leslie of the Gramophone Shop go my sincere thanks. Though we have sometimes worked together in making the selections, it is his knowledge of the field that has rendered this list possible. I have confined myself mainly to listening—though in so doing I have reaped a signal benefit. I have found that of the music which I thought I knew, some I had never really heard as I now know it can be played. I am therefore

On the Enjoyment of Music

doubly indebted for the help I have received, for inadvertently it has also served to broaden my musical horizon.

PAUL GRABBE

New York City
August, 1940.

Johann Sebastian Bach

BORN 1685 AT EISENACH, Germany, the son of a violinist, descendant of a line of musicians extending back over two hundred years. Became an orphan at ten and went to live with his brother who taught him to play the clavichord. At the time copied music surreptitiously at night with consequences later disastrous to his eyes. Studied at the Lyceum in Ohrdruf, and began composing for the organ at sixteen. Two years later started long musical career with a job as violinist in the ducal orchestra at Weimar. Thereafter held miscellaneous jobs as church organist, cantor, and, later, as court composer, marrying twice: first, at twenty-two, his cousin, Maria B. Bach, who bore him seven children; after her death, again, at thirty-six, Anna M. Wilcken, who bore him thirteen children. Went virtually blind in 1749 and died of a paralytic stroke the following year (aged 65) at Leipzig, Germany.

Johann Sebastian Bach

Bach's music has strength, simplicity, and great nobility of spirit. Its towering serenity; the outward ease of its most intricate design; the lofty fervor of its melodies—all of these make Bach's message stir responsive echoes in us all.

Two things stand out about Bach: first, the consistently high quality of his work (which fills sixty large volumes); second, the remarkably unanimous veneration accorded to him by musicians and music lovers throughout the Western World. This veneration is not unmixed with awe. For Bach is seen today for what he was—not a pioneer, but a great wizard, alone among musicians of any age to have achieved the feat of saying everything the art of his day made technically possible; of being, in addition, as vital in his message in the Twentieth Century as he was in the Eighteenth—"the most stupendous miracle in all music," to quote Wagner's words.

This attitude is relatively recent. Bach in his day was well known, but when he died, his music was neglected, almost forgotten, until Mendelssohn picked it up, and, with the performance of the *St. Matthew Passion*, in 1829, started its revival. (For other works of Bach, see *Recommended Recordings*).

Of Bach's sons, several achieved prominence in music: especially Johann Christian and Carl Philipp Emanuel. The latter, a founder of the modern school of piano playing, was also a pioneer of greatest importance in the development of the symphony.

Previously, the *fugue,* involving the presentation of a single tune, had been essentially the basis of musical structure. But through his bold experiments, Carl Philipp Emanuel created a blueprint of something else, the *symphony,* based on the presentation of two tunes, co-equal in importance.

It is from this blueprint that composers such as Haydn learned how to construct their symphonies—were able, in so doing, to lay a foundation sufficiently solid and definite to support the towering thought of a Beethoven.

Though overshadowed by the colossal stature of his father, Carl Philipp Emanuel was therefore more important to progress in music, although his compositions, as such, were less important. Without him, Haydn, eighteen years his junior, would probably not have written what he did. And without both, Beethoven would have been impossible, for each in turn had paved the way for his immediate successor and so enabled him to start where he left off.

BRANDENBURG CONCERTOS
DATE OF FIRST PERFORMANCE UNCERTAIN;
(PERHAPS 1721–22)

There once lived a young Prussian prince who spent a part of his time and a good deal of his money collecting music—in the manner that some people collect paintings or postage stamps. In the year 1719, this bachelor prince heard music performed by players attached to the household of a rival prince, and he was so impressed with the music of one of these—the capellmeister— that he commissioned him to write a set of six concertos, or compositions, for solo instruments with string orchestra accompaniment.

The name of this young prince was Christian Ludwig, Margraf of Brandenburg, and the musician he employed to write the concertos was Johann Sebastian Bach, then in his thirty-fourth year.

There is reason to believe that this assignment was not only welcomed by Bach, but regarded as of highest importance. It was his first major commission in the realm of secular music. It was also his long awaited chance to experiment in orchestral writing with such instruments as the French horn, trumpet, oboe, flute, etc. For although, in Bach's time, these instruments were used with the orchestra, singly or in groups, convention decreed that they be made to alternate with the *orchestra*—a word used to designate the strings only. But what Bach wanted to attempt was to make the orchestra and these instruments not "alternate" but "interpenetrate"; to have, in the words of Schweitzer, "the various tone-groups react on each other," in a continuously shifting mosaic of sound.

As in almost everything else he attempted, Bach not only succeeded in realizing his purpose but produced in these works music of great distinction and of unflagging inspiration.

In 1721 Bach finished the six (Brandenburg) concertos and sent them to the Margraf's house where they were duly stored away and, presumably, never played. All that is definitely known is that following Brandenburg's death, his musical library was sold in job lots and that Bach's concertos brought an equivalent of ten cents apiece. The manuscripts eventually found their way to the Royal Library in Berlin.

They were first printed in 1850, exactly one hundred years after the composer's death.

Johann Sebastian Bach

BRANDENBURG CONCERTO NO. 1
In F Major

SCORED FOR 1 VIOLIN, 1 BASSOON, 2 FRENCH
HORNS, 3 OBOES, WITH STRING ORCHESTRA AND
PIANO (ORIGINALLY HARPSICHORD)

This concerto contains more "solo" instruments than any of the others, and is thought
by some to have been Bach's favorite of the
six. Its movements are short, developed
mostly from one dominant theme.

GUIDE TO LISTENING

First Movement: Is marked by a mood of
spirited reserve, of vigor held in check.
Second Movement: Is distinguished by a
mood of solemn awe suggestive of the atmosphere of a cathedral. The oboe carries the
opening melody, echoed by the solo violin.
Thereafter the whole orchestra supports a
duet between these two instruments.
Third Movement: Is characterized by a care-
free good humor as of a country dance, with
the solo violin especially in evidence. After
a slowing up, as if to end, the music picks
up again and closes with a jolly flourish.
Fourth Movement: Is longer than the preceding and was added by Bach as a conces-
sion to the prevailing weakness in musical

circles for dance rhythms. Its mood, on the whole, is contemplative although its rhythms are those of a minuet and polacca—the latter a polonaise written in the Italian manner.

BRANDENBURG CONCERTO NO. 2
In F Major
SCORED FOR 1 TRUMPET, 1 FLUTE, 1 OBOE, 1 VIOLIN, WITH STRING ORCHESTRA AND PIANO (ORIGINALLY HARPSICHORD)

This concerto is more popular than the first. Its distinctive feature is that all four solo instruments—trumpet, flute, oboe, violin—are of high register, (custom at the time decreeing that the use of four solo instruments be subdivided among two high and two low instruments).

GUIDE TO LISTENING

First Movement: Is marked by an easy-flowing vitality which never relaxes.

Second Movement: Is characterized by a wistfulness of great emotional intensity. First the violin alone, then the violin and oboe take up the throbbing song.

Third Movement: Is marked by a contagious lightheartedness which glistens with gayety. The movement is fugal in construction, meaning that each instrument in turn picks up the original theme and projects it through the constantly moving tonal fabric.

BRANDENBURG CONCERTO NO. 3
In G Major
SCORED FOR STRING ORCHESTRA AND PIANO
(ORIGINALLY HARPSICHORD)

This concerto is the best known and probably the best liked of the series. Its distinctive feature is that Bach, in place of using wind instruments as solos, tried to get his contrasting tonal combinations by subdividing the strings in three groups of three instruments each, and pitting one against the other.

GUIDE TO LISTENING

First Movement: Is marked by a busy-like precision, the music hastening along but in a stately way. (It is believed that Bach meant the two chords that appear after the ending as substitutes for the customary slow movement that should have followed.)

Second Movement: Is a fast moving jig, characterized by great vitality. It's invigorating briskness is maintained with superb skill.

Johann Sebastian Bach

BRANDENBURG CONCERTO NO. 4
In G Major
SCORED FOR 1 VIOLIN, 2 FLUTES WITH STRING
ORCHESTRA AND PIANO (ORIGINALLY
HARPSICHORD)

This concerto is perhaps the most masterly and beautiful of the set. Its distinctive feature is the prominent role allotted to the solo violin.

GUIDE TO LISTENING

First Movement: Is marked by a steady-going forward motion, requiring expert playing on the part of the soloists since most of the work falls on their shoulders.

Second Movement: Is characterized by a mood of majestic gravity, the weighty question propounded by the orchestra being not so much answered as echoed by the flutes. The violin helps out mournfully in this musical discourse, which ends on a note of expectancy.

Third Movement: Is rapid and vigorous, and in the music lurk overtones of merriment. The movement is fugal (see third movement of Second Concerto) with the exuberant melody first voiced by the violas.

Johann Sebastian Bach

BRANDENBURG CONCERTO NO. 5
In D Major
SCORED FOR 1 VIOLIN, 1 FLUTE WITH STRING
ORCHESTRA AND PIANO (ORIGINALLY
HARPSICHORD)

This concerto is one of the best liked of the set; for, in the regard it shows for the individuality of the different instruments, it is a definite forerunner of the style of writing in a modern concerto.

GUIDE TO LISTENING

First Movement: Is marked by a refreshing lyricism with a touch of wistfulness here and there. After a bold opening, we hear the piano answered by the flute and violin. The movement displays great inventiveness, ingenuity, and beauty.

Second Movement: Is characterized by quiet simplicity. It is restricted to the solo instruments—violin, flute, with piano—the orchestra remaining silent throughout.

Third Movement: Is marked by a sprightly tunefulness suggestive of the country dance —an Irish jig, perhaps. The violin and flute intone the catchy melody which skips lightly from instrument to instrument in truly delightful fashion.

Johann Sebastian Bach

BRANDENBURG CONCERTO NO. 6
In B-Flat Major

SCORED FOR 2 VIOLAS DA BRACCIA (OR "ARM-VIOLAS," NOW OBSOLETE), 2 VIOLAS DA GAMBA (OR "LEG-VIOLAS"), 1 'CELLO, 1 DOUBLE-BASS, AND PIANO (ORIGINALLY HARPSICHORD)

The distinctive feature of this concerto is the employment of the da Gamba violas; for the tone of this instrument, which is a precursor of the 'cello, is yet distinct from the tone of the modern 'cello or viola. (The da Braccia viola parts, however, are today usually assigned to modern violas.)

GUIDE TO LISTENING

First Movement: Is marked by a certain mysterious serenity, felt in spite of the peculiarly halting forward motion of the music.

Second Movement: Is characterized by a feeling of grave solemnity, religious in mood. The music develops as an extended duet between violas and 'cellos.

Third Movement: Is suggestive of a square dance, charmingly varied, delightfully dignified. The music unfolds with a quietly self-contained precision and culminates in a vigorously stated final appearance of the theme.

[11]

Ludwig van Beethoven

BORN 1770 IN BONN on the Rhine. Was taught the violin and clavier at three by his father, a singer in the Electoral choir. At eight played his first concert. Within a year or two is said to have composed a Funeral Cantata for a deceased friend of the family. At eleven, already displaying great gifts, substituted in church for the organist Neefe who was his teacher. At seventeen, managed somehow (the family was very poor) to visit Vienna and take a few lessons from Mozart. Thereafter, through teaching and playing, began to make useful contacts with influential people. At eighteen, through prior death of mother and drunkenness of father, became responsible for two younger brothers and a sister.

Had as yet composed little worth mentioning, but, being a remarkable extemporizer on piano and organ, at twenty-two was sent at the Elector's expense, to study music in

Vienna. Here met many patrons of the arts and began to enjoy not only growing social and financial success, but also increasing fame as a composer. From then on, afflicted with growing deafness which culminated in a complete loss of hearing when he was in his late forties, became increasingly suspicious and cantankerous as a man; as a composer, increasingly misunderstood. Died 1827 (aged 57) in Vienna, Austria, defiantly shaking his fist at the sky during a thunderstorm.

Characteristic of much of Beethoven's music is the feeling it gives of having so much of urgent import it must communicate. Even in its moods of robust lyricism or tender gravity we sense in it a certain inexorable quality—a depth and width and a titanic drive not found elsewhere in music.

Though the quality of Beethoven's output is uneven, his work, at its best, makes him a dominant figure in music. For what Beethoven did was to democratize music. He seized music by the collar, jerked it down from its privileged state as something manufactured for the entertainment of princes, shook it free of its formal politeness, and replaced it squarely on its feet—an art transformed, with a ring universal, expressing the whole range of emotions of flesh and blood humanity.

Ludwig van Beethoven

SYMPHONY NO. 3
In E-Flat Major, Op. 55 (*Eroica*)
FIRST PERFORMANCE: VIENNA, APRIL 7, 1805

Beethoven was just past thirty when symptoms of oncoming deafness began to manifest themselves so clearly that it became impossible for him to ignore them or conceal them from others.

Once, while strolling with Beethoven, so Ries relates, he called the composer's attention to a shepherd "piping very agreeably in the woods on a flute. . . ." Beethoven listened intently, but he heard nothing; and when his companion, realizing the truth, hastened to assure him that the piping had ceased, the composer "became extremely quiet and morose."

During this period Beethoven went through some bad moments. He was living in a secluded suburb of Vienna, under conditions ideal for work, but he was struggling against accepting the reality of his deafness, and this struggle often plunged him into moods of darkest depression. Finally, with a great effort, he threw off this torturing mood and threw himself into the composition of his Third Symphony.

[14]

Ludwig van Beethoven

At the time young Bonaparte was initiating great changes in Europe, and it was to him that the democratically-minded Beethoven dedicated the Symphony. But when he learned that the republican First Consul—enemy of Kings and, to Beethoven, a symbol of human emancipation—had proclaimed himself Emperor, the composer tore up the first page of the score in a great fit of disillusioned rage. On a fresh page he wrote in large letters: "Simphonia Eroica," to which he later added—"composed to celebrate the memory of a great man."

The towering stature of the work; its tempestuous power; the episode of its re-dedication—all of these have tempted commentators to see the Symphony as a portrait of Napoleon. It is more likely, however, as Sir George Grove shrewdly points out, that the "gigantic hero whom Beethoven believed himself to be portraying . . . was certainly more himself than Bonaparte."

GUIDE TO LISTENING

First Movement: Two crashing chords introduce the main theme, heard in the 'cellos. A second, quieter theme follows, whereupon the music undergoes extensive development, steadily gaining in momentum and power. *Second Movement:* The violins softly open this movement which is one of the two most famous funeral marches in music (the other is Chopin's). The oboe repeats the theme, and the music slowly grows in power until it reaches, as Lawrence Gilman remarks, a truly "titanic quality" of restrained intensity. *Third Movement:* In this contagiously animated scherzo, we are lifted right up and carried along on the bright wings of a lively tune, believed to have been an Austrian folk song which Beethoven picked up somewhere near Vienna.

Fourth Movement: This movement consists, in the main, of a set of variations on a theme of which Beethoven was presumed to have been very fond, for he used it in several other compositions.

OVERTURE TO "LEONORE" NO. 3
Op. 72
FIRST PERFORMANCE: VIENNA, MARCH 29, 1806

Beethoven composed only one opera, the seldom performed *Fidelio* of which he said shortly before his death: "Of all my children this one cost me the worst birth-pangs; brought me most sorrow; is also the one that is most dear to me." He spoke truly. On no other work did he expend so much toil

[16]

or lavish so much loving care. He made ten different attempts to perfect one of the choruses. One of the songs he revised eighteen times. The opera's overture he re-wrote four times—giving us four distinct versions and generating much controversy among musical scholars. (Some insist that the work known as the *Leonore Overture No. 1* is the earliest version of all; others regard it as a later effort, made "light" for a special performance in Prague.)

Definitely established are the following facts: that *Leonore Overture No. 2* was the one written for the initial performance of the opera in 1805. The demands made by this work on players of woodwind instruments seem to have been considered too taxing, and so, in 1806, Beethoven recast the music into what is now known as *Leonore Overture No. 3.* This process of revision seems to have absorbed him to such an extent that he tightened the work all around, thereby unwittingly increasing rather than lessening its playing difficulty.

Therefore, in 1814, still anxious to provide a really serviceable overture for the opera, Beethoven wrote a less exacting, fourth version. It was called the *Fidelio Overture,* though not without opposition from the composer who still preferred the title *Leonore.*

Ludwig van Beethoven

As will be recalled, Leonore is the name of the opera's heroine who, by disguising herself as a man and finding employment in the prison where her husband, Floristan, has been unjustly thrown by a political rival, is able to intercede in time and save her husband from death.

GUIDE TO LISTENING

A slow introduction, grave in mood, gives a picture of Floristan confined in his prison cell. The music paints the dramatic emotions of the prisoner as he reflects on his fate and recalls his life as a free man. A trumpet call heralds the approach of the Governor whose timely appearance will save Floristan. Increasing in suspense, the music keeps us on edge until the moment when a triumphant fanfare marks the prisoner's jubilation at his release.

CONCERTO (VIOLIN AND ORCHESTRA)
In D Major, Op. 61
FIRST PERFORMANCE: VIENNA, DECEMBER 23, 1806

While this Concerto was being written, the Austrian countryside was overrun with French troops. Officers and soldiers of the invading army were quartered everywhere, even in the house where Beethoven lived. These Frenchmen often importuned the composer with requests that he play for them; they delighted in teasing him with hints of possible arrest if he refused. This annoyed Beethoven greatly, but in spite of these interruptions, he continued working on the Concerto, now conceded to be the greatest work of its kind.

GUIDE TO LISTENING

First Movement: The work opens in a pensive mood, its main theme ushered in by four raps on the kettledrums—said to have suggested themselves to Beethoven by a neighbor's knocks on the door while he was at work late one night. A long and dazzling passage for the solo instrument, playing alone, is heard just before the end.

Second Movement: Is mysteriously contemplative; one is almost tempted to say, deeply pious; the solo violin providing a running commentary on the main theme.

Third Movement: The principal melody is a good-humored folk dance dressed up in symphonic garb. Again, toward the end, the solo instrument plays alone; then the music surges to an exultant end.

Ludwig van Beethoven

OVERTURE TO "CORIOLANUS"
Op. 62
FIRST PERFORMANCE: VIENNA, MARCH 1807

Late in 1806 the manager of the Court
Theater in Vienna was replaced by a board
of directors, and to this board Beethoven
addressed a petition seeking an appointment
as composer to the Theater. The answer
never came. The new management was unwilling to grant the petition and take a
chance with the unpredictable Beethoven
whose growing deafness was well known.
But it was also unwilling to refuse it and
thereby offend the composer. So the management stalled and, while it stalled, Beethoven, as if to prove his talent for dramatic
composition, and not unlikely with the management of the Court Theater in mind, applied himself to the writing of the *Overture .
Coriolanus* (after a play by H. J. Collin).

The story of the play concerns itself with
the Roman warrior Coriolanus. Impeached
and condemned to banishment by the Ro-
mans, he takes refuge among the Volsciens,
but returns to destroy Rome as a general of
the Volscian army. To stop him, the Ro-
mans send out his wife and mother who

entreat Coriolanus to spare Rome. This he finally does at the cost of his life, for he is killed by his soldiers.

GUIDE TO LISTENING

The work opens with long-held, single tones in the strings, drowned several times by resounding, angry chords which usher in a sullen, agitated melody—all suggestive of Coriolanus' vainglorious pride, his stubborn resistance to his wife's and his mother's entreaties that he spare Rome. The passionate second theme suggests the struggle of Coriolanus' better self as it reasserts itself, forcing him finally to yield.

SYMPHONY NO. 5
In C Minor, Op. 67
FIRST PERFORMANCE: VIENNA, DECEMBER 22, 1808

A young musician who met Beethoven in 1808 spoke of the composer in a letter to his sister as follows: "He is a singular man . . . as singular as are his compositions . . . very childlike and sincere . . . a great lover of truth . . . but in this he often goes much too far . . ."

The accuracy of this judgment need not be doubted. At a rehearsal, two or three months

after the letter was written, Beethoven stopped
the music to correct the members of the orchestra on some detail of their playing. Undoubtedly what he told them was the truth—
but whatever it was he said, he so outraged
the musicians that they refused to play under
his leadership or even to continue the rehearsal in his presence. Chagrined but forced
to yield, Beethoven found himself banished
to an anteroom adjoining the main hall,
there to pace moodily back and forth while
the orchestra rehearsed that strange new
work—his Fifth Symphony.

GUIDE TO LISTENING

First Movement: Three short notes in the
strings, urgently repeated, coming to rest on
a lower fourth note, open the work. On this
combination of notes, perhaps the most famous in all music, Beethoven builds a monumental structure which unfolds with intensely dramatic grandeur.

Second Movement: In contrast to the terrify-
ing struggle that rages through the first
movement, the music here is almost calm, or,
shall we say, sober. It is also easy-flowing, and
profoundly eloquent in its directness.

Third Movement: Muttering deeply in the
depths, the strings at once create a mood of
hushed anticipation. Piercing this sombre

curtain, the voice of the French horn utters a clarion call, insistent and not unlike the passage that opened the Symphony. Again the strings mutter darkly, and again the clarion call is heard, this time in the strings. From here on the music grows in savage intensity, but subsides again toward the end of the movement to a mood brooding, and mysterious.

Fourth Movement: The music bursts forth in a triumphant cry which seems to soar through all space—a cry pregnant, as Lawrence Gilman has said "with the greatness of the indomitable human soul."

SYMPHONY NO. 6
In F Major, Op. 68 (*Pastoral*)
FIRST PERFORMANCE: VIENNA, DECEMBER 22, 1808

Fifteen years after he had composed his Sixth Symphony, Beethoven went for a stroll with Schindler, his biographer, in the wooded suburbs of Vienna where he had composed the work. Concerning this walk, Schindler writes:

"Beethoven constantly stopped and let his gaze roam happily over the landscape. Then, seating himself on a tuft of grass and letting his body rest against an elm, he asked me if any yellowhammers could be heard in the trees. I assured him that around us all was quite still. Then turning to me he said: 'Here I composed the Scene by the Brook, and the yellowhammers up there, the nightingales, the quails and cuckoos round about, composed with me.'"

In his *Pastoral Symphony*, Beethoven went directly to Nature for his inspiration. He emerged with music mellow and endearing, breathing a freshness of Spring, full of tender gravity, of relaxed loveliness.

Enlarging on the subtitles of each movement which were provided by the composer, Hector Berlioz has written what is probably the best literary guide to the enjoyment of the Symphony. Too long to quote, these notes are given here in free transcription.

GUIDE TO LISTENING

First Movement—"Serene Impressions awakened by Arrival in the Country": The vapors of a summer dawn envelop the countryside. Shepherds appear here and there. Their pipes are heard gently from afar. Perfumed morning breezes float through the coolness of early morn, dissipating the mists. Green fields and pastures are revealed to the eye. On the horizon flocks of birds streak the sky.

Under the caressing glory of the rising sun, Nature slowly comes to life.

Second Movement—By the Brook: We lie in the tall grasses of a clearing in the woods and listen to the waters of a gently rippling brook. A contemplative mood envelops us and seems to carry us into the distance of the woods from whose brooding depths the voice of the cuckoo is heard calling softly.

Third Movement—A Merry Gathering of Country Folk: We are in the midst of a group of merry-making German peasants. They dance and drink, and their laughter echoes through the countryside. Suddenly the dull mutterings of a thunderstorm are heard, interrupting the dance and sending everyone scurrying to shelter.

Fourth Movement—The Tempest: Gusts of wind, laden with rain, rip through the countryside. The storm approaches, swells, bursts forth in all its fury. We listen to its thundering detonations and watch its torrents of rain.

Fifth Movement—Shepherd's Song—Glad and Thankful Feelings after the Storm: The storm has passed and the sky is rapidly clearing. From afar we hear rustic songs of the village folk. These gentle melodies float through the countryside, their accents of gratitude bringing peace to the soul.

Ludwig van Beethoven

CONCERTO (PIANO AND ORCHESTRA) NO. 5

In E-Flat Major, Op. 73 (*Emperor*)

FIRST PERFORMANCE: PROBABLY LEIPZIG, NOVEMBER 28, 1811

While this Concerto was being written, Vienna was besieged and taken by the French; and—so the story goes—when the noise of the shooting and cannonading grew too intense, Beethoven took refuge from it in a cellar. There, with a pillow over his head, he went on with the composition of his concerto—a work whose proud distinction was later to earn the popular designation "Emperor."

GUIDE TO LISTENING

First Movement: The three opening, sweeping chords in the orchestra, separated from one another by brief rhapsodic excursions in the piano, at once make clear the imposing character of the work. For some time after this the orchestra occupies itself with a lengthy introduction. It finally yields the spotlight to the piano, and the movement at last gets into its stride.

Second Movement: This movement is very

[26]

different. Here the mood is subdued and solemn—devotional is perhaps the right word. The piano presently sounds a lovely melody, each note of which sparkles like a jewel. *Third Movement:* Is lively with a vigor full-blooded and gruffly good-natured. The main theme is a catchy tune, and the piano and orchestra make the most of it.

OVERTURE TO GOETHE'S "EGMONT"
Op. 84
FIRST PERFORMANCE: VIENNA, MAY 24, 1810

An interesting sidelight on this Overture is that it was played in 1935 at a request program of the radio audience, to celebrate the two-hundredth Sunday afternoon broadcast of the New York Philharmonic. The voting of the radio audience revealed Beethoven, Brahms, Wagner, Tchaikowsky, in the order named, as the most popular composers of the past.

The *Egmont Overture,* together with some incidental music for the play, similarly named, was written by Beethoven to order for a performance at the Vienna Court Theater.

The story of this play, taking a page from the dark early history of the Netherlands

[27]

then under the oppressive rule of Spain, tells of the revolt of the people against the harsh rule of Spain's regent, the Duke of Alva. The Duke lays a trap for the idealistic but weak would-be liberator, Egmont, who falls into it and perishes on the scaffold—whereupon the people arise and overthrow the tyrant.

GUIDE TO LISTENING

"The Overture," says Dr. Leopold Damrosch, "begins with an outcry . . . uttered by the entire nation. Then follow heavy, determined chords which seem to press down the very life of the people. . . . Only the all-pervading woe remains . . . sounded . . . first by the oboe. . . ." A sudden quickening of the music, perhaps symbolic of Egmont's awakening to his countrymen's need for leadership in their hour of trial, is followed by the reappearance of the dark, foreboding chords, which seem to presage Egmont's hesitancy, his capture by the tyrant, and his doom.

Thus the drama unfolds until, toward the end, insurrection breaks loose. Irresistibly it rolls onward through the streets, swelling into a loud cry of victory at the downfall of the tyrant.

Ludwig van Beethoven

SYMPHONY NO. 7
In A Major, Op. 92
FIRST PERFORMANCE: VIENNA, DECEMBER 8, 1813

About the time when Beethoven was completing his Seventh Symphony, he met Goethe at a Bohemian spa, and the two went for a walk together. During this walk, Beethoven, whom Goethe regarded "with mingled admiration and dread" proceeded to harangue his companion on a favorite topic of his. The great of this world, he said, are not kings and princes, but writers like you; composers like myself. Kings and princes cannot create great minds, even though they may give away titles, bestow decorations, or make privy councillors. . . .

Here Beethoven caught himself, remembering that Goethe was a privy councillor. He was about to change the subject when he saw "the whole Imperial family approaching from a distance. Goethe let go of my hand," he later wrote, "and took his place with the crowd by the side of the road. In vain did I plead with him. He would not budge an inch. I pulled my hat down on my head, buttoned up my coat, and pushed my way through the crowd. Princes and

courtiers made room for me to pass. The
Duke Rudolph raised his hat. The Empress
bowed to me first. . . . Amused, I watched
the procession as it moved past Goethe. He
stood there, hat in hand, bowing deeply. I
took him to task for it pretty severely . . ."
(something Goethe never forgot or quite for-
gave).

Such was the man who wrote this Symphony—a composition referred to by some
of his contemporaries, who could not understand him, as the work of a drunkard.

GUIDE TO LISTENING

First Movement: The voices of oboe, clarinet,
French horn, and bassoon are heard succes-
sively, each emerging from under one of the
four introductory crashing chords. This
material is repeated in various ways before
the main theme of the movement is reached.
This theme is introduced by the flute, and
its vigorous rhythm is thereafter kept up relentlessly.

Second Movement: Glowing deeply yet mar-
vellously restrained in the pensive sadness it
conveys is this music—unsurpassed as an example of what a really great composer is able
to achieve with relatively simple means. Unhurriedly it unfolds; and again as in the first

movement, a single rhythmic pattern is maintained.

Third Movement: Is rapid and irresistibly vigorous. On this brilliant display of exuberance, another more solemn mood intrudes itself twice. But the vigorous mood triumphs, for the hymn-like melody is drowned at the end by a succession of five mighty chords.

Fourth Movement: Is savage, almost frenzied; and in listening to it one is perforce reminded of Carlyle's hero Ram Dass who had "enough fire in his belly to burn up the entire world;"—so irresistibly boisterous is this finale, so furiously powerful in its forward sweep.

SYMPHONY NO. 9

In D Minor, with Final Chorus on Schiller's *Ode to Joy* Op. 125, (Popularly Known as the *Choral Symphony*)

FIRST PERFORMANCE: VIENNA, MAY 7, 1824

Beethoven had a habit of noting down musical ideas in sketchbooks which he carried around with him; of re-working these ideas, again and again, sometimes over a period of years, until, finally satisfied with their content, he would give them their final expression. Most of Beethoven's works passed through this exacting process, and the Ninth Symphony was no exception—a fact rather upsetting to the "stroke of genius" view of creative endeavor.

Notations and melodies intended for the Ninth Symphony date as far back as 1817. They make clear that Beethoven had the work in mind at least six years, thinking about it and tightening its ideas even while attending to the execution of other, lesser works.

When the Symphony was finally ready, its initial performance drew an enthusiastic response. To this, Beethoven at first did not respond. Stone deaf, completely unaware of the ovation he was receiving, he stood there on the conductor's stand, his back to the audience, until one of the soloists took him by the sleeve and pushed him gently around. This incident, touching and rather pitiful, seems to have electrified the audience, for in it were many of Beethoven's friends and admirers; but it may be doubted if many of those present really perceived the greatness of this unprecedented symphony with voices in it.

Not until the latter part of the nineteenth century did the work—perhaps the most monumental work in all music—make any appreciable headway, and then largely through the ministrations of Richard Wagner who took it upon himself, through repeated performances, to make the *Symphony* better known to the public at large.

GUIDE TO LISTENING

First Movement: The work opens with a mysterious rustling in the strings through which we hear the voices of different instruments, as if propounding questions. These are scarcely over when we begin to sense, dimly at first but with increasing certainty, that we are in the presence of something that has depth and width and titanic power. In accents subdued but more and more agitated the movement unfolds, its first theme appropriately likened by some to the pounding of a giant anvil. Suspense hangs over this music, and stress; and its occasional oases of relative tranquility are quickly swallowed by stormy outbursts from the entire orchestra.

Second Movement: Three spirited ejaculations by the orchestra—the third preceded by a loud imitation on the kettledrums—and the music rushes irresistibly forward. Its exhilarating rhythm, wild yet somehow jolly, conjures visions of a giant skipping merrily along. A breathing spell that is gently lyrical is provided by a contrasting middle section.

Third Movement: This is the slow movement of the *Symphony*—lovely, pleading, restrained in its principal melodies of which Hector Berlioz has said: "As for the beauty of these melodies, the infinite grace of the ornaments that envelop them . . . the tenderness, dreamy religious feeling they express—if my prose could but give an approximate idea of them, music would have found a rival in written speech. . . ."

Fourth Movement: The last movement starts clamorously, as though in a mood of militant defiance. This furious opening is followed immediately by brief snatches from the preceding three movements. Sir Donald F. Toby, one of the most scholarly students of Beethoven, has this to say on the subject:

". . . Beethoven's plan is to remind us of the first three movements . . . and to reject them one by one as failing to attain the joy in which he believes. After all three have been rejected, a new theme is to appear . . . hailed and sung as the hymn of joy."

This new theme is presently introduced, at first tentatively by the 'cellos and violas. These are joined by the violins, finally by the entire orchestra. Up to this point the singers have been silent, but now the baritone enters with the words: "O, friends, not these tones! Let us take up a more joyous strain." Whereupon the entire chorus joins in; and now, the triumphant accents of the *Ode to Joy* burst forth upon us—music of transcendental and triumphant gladness.

Trumpet

Hector Berlioz

BORN 1803 AT LA COTE-SAINT-ANDRÉ in South-western France, the son of a physician. Though as a child definitely inclined toward music, at eighteen was sent to study medicine in Paris—where he spent most of his time studying music instead. Nevertheless obtained his degree from the Medical School before entering the Paris Conservatory. At twenty-seven, won the coveted Prix de Rome, but his father disinherited him. Twice disappointed in love, married the actress Henrietta Smithson at twenty-nine, but later re-married, meanwhile waging a ceaseless struggle for recognition. Died 1869 (aged 65) in Paris.

Berlioz' music, at its best, rises to rare heights of stormy grandeur; at its worst, it is downright vulgar. Its friends point to its dramatic power, the glowing intensity of its melodies. Others, less well disposed, say it is longwinded, charge it with sensationalism.

All agree that it is the work of a genius, now acknowledged as the father of modern orchestration and as one of France's greatest composers. (For other works by Berlioz, see *Recommended Recordings*.)

SYMPHONIE FANTASTIQUE
Op. 14-A (From *Episode in the Life of an Artist*)
FIRST PERFORMANCE: PARIS, DECEMBER 5, 1830

Berlioz—turbulent, erratic, prone to falling extravagantly in love and given to wild exaggerations of his passions before falling out of love again—went in 1827 to the theater and there saw for the first time the young Irish actress, Henrietta Smithson, in the role of Ophelia. The effect of this visual impact on the twenty-five-year-old composer, judging from his own testimony, was that of a thunderbolt. He left the theater "vowing solemnly never again to expose himself to such an emotional bombardment"—but he did.

Now it would be natural for the average young man, under similar circumstances, to make some effort at once toward placing the object of such overpowering love within the custody of his arms—or, at the very least, to clear the way for an early meeting. Not so

Berlioz. With a view to paying a proper tribute to the young actress; incidentally, also as a means of bringing himself to her attention, he undertook to arrange a concert devoted exclusively to his own works—an unprecedented idea for an unrecognized composer—but it is doubtful if Henrietta ever heard of the event.

Consumed with passion for the young actress, his efforts to bring himself to her attention having temporarily failed, Berlioz retired to the country. Later, while in his twenty-sixth year, now considerably less enamored, he gave expression to his unrequited love by writing that curious work of self-dramatization, the *Fantastic Symphony*, to which he appended some explanatory notes, quoted in abridged form below.

Preamble—"A young musician, morbidly inclined . . . poisons himself with opium . . . in a fit of lovesick despair. . . . The doze, too weak to cause death, plunges him into a heavy stupor accompanied by many extraordinary visions. . . . The beloved woman herself becomes for him a melody . . . which he hears everywhere."

GUIDE TO LISTENING

First Movement—Dreams, Passions: "First he recalls that uneasy state of mind . . . which he experienced before he met her . . . then the volcanic love with which she suddenly inspired him . . . his moments of anxiety, of jealous fury. . . ."

Second Movement—A Ball: "He sees his beloved during a ball, at a gay and brilliant party. . . ."

Third Movement—Scene in the Fields: "The playing of two shepherds one summer evening in the country . . . restores his calm. . . . But she appears again . . . and his heart stops beating. . . . What if she has betrayed him. . . ."

Fourth Movement—March to the Scaffold: "He dreams that he has killed his beloved, is condemned to death. The procession moves forward to the strains of a march, alternately sombre and wild. . . . As it nears the scaffold, momentarily a vision of his beloved reappears. . . ."

Fifth Movement—Witches Sabbath: "Now he sees himself in frightful company—ghosts, magicians, monsters—who have come to mourn over him. Briefly he hears the beloved melody, but it is transformed, vulgar, grotesque. . . . Lost is her shyness, her nobility. . . . **She joins in the infernal orgy. . . .**"

Hector Berlioz

EXCERPTS FROM "THE DAMNATION OF FAUST"

Op. 24

FIRST PERFORMANCE: PARIS, DECEMBER 6, 1846

Greatly impressed with Goethe's *Faust*, Berlioz undertook to set this masterpiece to music. He used a chorus, orchestra, and four principal singers, chose the salient points of the poem, and retouched the whole to suit his own fancy. The result amazed his contemporaries, bored some, and shocked quite a few.

The music, in the words of Samuel Chotzinoff, "is Berlioz at his best; startlingly sincere in a musician whose every musical breath was a conscious 'effort.' It has tenderness, poignant grief, and real warmth." The work, though seldom produced, is kept from oblivion through the frequent playing of several excerpts by symphony orchestras throughout the world.

GUIDE TO LISTENING

Minuet of the Will-o-the Wisps: Woodwinds introduce this fluttering minuet, picturing three gleaming spirits which, at the command of Mephistopheles, execute a picturesque dance under Marguerite's window.

Dance of the Sylphs: This dainty waltz pictures several Sylphs executing a dance near Faust who lies asleep on the banks of a river.

Hungarian ("Rakoczy") March: Originally, this rousing march had no connection with Faust. It was written for a concert in Hungary, but its success prompted Berlioz to incorporate it in the work, much to the annoyance of the German public which resented having its Goethe tampered with. Unconcerned, Berlioz invented for it a special scene in which Faust watches the passage of the Hungarian army.

Oboe

Georges Bizet

BORN 1838 AT PARIS, the son of a singing teacher. As a child displayed a startling gift for music and was admitted to the Paris Conservatory when barely nine years old. At nineteen, by winning the much coveted Prix de Rome, gained from the French Government a five year subsidy which took him to Italy. In subsequent years, earned a meager living in Paris through every form of hack work, at the same time composing but always falling just short of success. Died 1875 (aged 38) at Paris, three months after the premiere of *Carmen* which was to become an international favorite.

Bizet's musical speech has the dramatic opulence of a tropical sunset. Indeed, his music on the whole is a strange mixture of the exotic with the melodramatic, for it is usually vibrant, colorful, and lustful. Yet its gayety, as Nietzsche has said, "is African; destiny hangs over it."

SUITE NO. 1 FROM L'ARLÉSIENNE
FIRST PERFORMANCE: PARIS, OCTOBER 1, 1872

When Bizet was depressed he sometimes
spoke of music as "a splendid art, but a sad
trade." He had reference to the endless
drudgery which was his cross, sapping his
strength and driving him to a premature
end. In spite of this he found time to compose. When he was thirty-three he wrote to
order twenty-seven pieces of music for *L'Arlésienne,* a play by Daudet.

The story of the play concerns the dismal
fate of the young peasant Frederi who falls
in love with a girl from Arles, attempts to
quell his passion for her because she has
strayed from the path of virtue, but finally
kills himself by jumping from a garret window.

GUIDE TO LISTENING

Prelude: This music, introducing the play,
depicts the impassioned Frederi, and his
simpleton brother, the Innocent.

Minuet and Adagietto: This music follows
a secondary theme of the play—the patient
and tender love of the aged pair, Balthazar
and Mere Renaud.

Danse Provencale and Carillon: This depicts
a rustic celebration in Frederi's village.

Alexander Borodin

BORN 1833 AT ST. PETERSBURG, Russia, the illegitimate son of a Georgian nobleman. Set forth early in pursuit of his two loves—science and music. At twenty-two received his degree from the Academy of Medicine and Surgery at the capital and embarked on a career as a chemist, composing fitfully in his spare time. During the years that followed was very active as a college teacher, wrote eight important books on chemistry and at the same time achieved an even greater name as a composer. Died of a heart ailment 1887 (aged 54) at St. Petersburg, Russia.

Borodin's music alternates between tender lyricism and barbaric strength, displaying a special tendency toward melodies of Asiatic cast. Most salient is the fact that although this music, in its outward form, is Western, in spirit it has a true ring of the East. Its influence has been far-reaching, notably on Debussy, Sibelius, Stravinsky. Of Borodin's other works, note his opera *Prince Igor* and other works listed under *Recommended Recordings.*

SYMPHONY NO. 2
In B Minor
FIRST PERFORMANCE: ST. PETERSBURG, FEBRUARY 14, 1877

It took Borodin six years to complete his Second Symphony, for his pressing duties as a scientist, involving lectures at the Academy, laboratory work, faculty meetings, and examinations, were a constant hindrance to his work as a composer.

"Days, weeks, months, whole winters go by," he complained, "without a chance to get seriously to work. Not that I could not find some hours a day, but that I have no leisure of mind and cannot get away from concerns that have nothing to do with music. . . . In the winter I can compose only when I am sick. When I am tied down to the house . . . my head splitting, my eyes burning, and I have to blow my nose all the time—then I give myself up to composing. So, my friends, wish me not good health. Say instead: I hope you are ill!"

The first performance of the Symphony

had to be postponed for a month to give Borodin time to find parts of the score which he had mislaid. Unable to find the missing parts, he had to rescore them breathlessly from memory while sick in bed.

GUIDE TO LISTENING

First Movement: The Symphony opens with a melody unmistakably Asiatic—bold, elemental, suggestive of rugged expanses on which roam primitive, barbaric people. The second theme, introduced by the 'cellos, is warmer, more lyrical, and Russian rather than Asiatic in spirit.

Second Movement: A rapid repetition of a single note on the French horn dominates the music, lurking incessantly in the background as an accompaniment to the agitated rhythms suggestive of a barbaric dance.

Third Movement: First a clarinet is heard with harp accompaniment. It is quickly followed by the French horn which sings a song of unutterable loneliness, transporting us, it would seem, to some spot on the prairie, far removed from civilization.

Fourth Movement: A Tartar dance, fiery in mood, fierce in its thrusting power, is heard soon after the start. The music subsides briefly, then rushes us head-on to a vigorous end.

Johannes Brahms

BORN 1833 AT HAMBURG, Germany, the son of
a double-bass player. Gave his first piano
recital at fifteen, at which time he was already composing. Studied with various teachers until, at twenty, attracted the attention
of Robert Schumann who both helped and
embarrassed the young composer by pro-
claiming him the new messiah of music.
Following years of hard-won recognition,
Brahms settled to a quiet bachelor existence,
composing, playing, conducting, and gaining,
year by year, an ever wider reputation as one
of Germany's greatest symphonists. Died of
cancer 1893 (aged 63) at Vienna, Austria.

There is something essentially sturdy and
substantial about the music of Brahms—
something which partakes of the quality of a
main course. It is, in short, solid fare, but
the listening satisfaction it affords is solid
too. For the musical speech of Brahms is
cast in the grand manner—rich in melody,

overflowing with mellowness and humanity, yet delivering itself of its message with a certain epic directness that finds no counterpart in music. Of Brahms' many compositions note especially his beautiful *Lieder;* his *Clarinet Quintet* and his *Trio for violin, piano, and horn.*

SYMPHONY NO. 1
In C Minor, Op. 68
FIRST PERFORMANCE: CARLSRUHE, NOVEMBER 4, 1876

For nearly sixteen years Brahms let his First Symphony germinate in his mind, regarding such an undertaking as a responsibility not to be taken lightly. When he finally finished it, he was forty-three, already famous, and not a little eccentric.

Brahms at that time was not yet the patriarchal looking man with flowing beard that he became in later years. By disposition, though, he was already gruff, often selfishly unsociable. Strange man this Brahms—shy, kindly, on occasion even tender, yet just as frequently self-willed, sarcastic, even cruel; a stubborn man with a wide streak of coarseness in his fibre, and yet a man of deeply human understanding and great tact. It is related that when Mrs. Strauss, the wife of

the waltz king, asked Brahms for an auto-
graph, he penned the first few measures of
the *Blue Danube* and scribbled underneath:
"unfortunately not by me—J. Brahms."

The First Symphony of Brahms, truly an
epic work in structure and emotional intensity, aroused more controversy than enthusiasm when first performed. Currently,
it stands close to the top as a concert favorite.

GUIDE TO LISTENING

First Movement: The opening pages of this
work are laden with storm, swelling with a
grandeur deep rolling and angry. The mood
lightens as the movement progresses, but not
for long. In restless yet majestic accents the
music carries us on a rising wave of tone
which ebbs quickly and passes into stillness.

Second Movement: Deeply reflective is the
prevailing mood of this movement; deeply
tinged, too, with sadness—a sadness of brooding melancholy such as we may experience
when watching a strife-torn world. This is
neither despair nor personal tragedy, for the
music seems to retain a calm, philosophic
grip on reality.

Third Movement: The voice of the clarinet
opens this movement with a melody of charming daintiness—a melody, as Geiringer puts

it, which "seems to smile through its tears." Through the tonal fabric a second melody emerges, then a third, but the mood remains that of delicate and sunny good humor.

Fourth Movement: Intense, mysterious is the first theme, uttered by the violins. The mood is that of foreboding, and it darkens perceptibly until, after a dramatic roll, there emerges a lovely melody, broadly uttered and serene. When it has spent itself, there is a short, preparatory interlude—then there bursts forth on us a song of overwhelming gladness, equaled in its mood of rejoicing only by the *Ode to Joy* in the last movement of *Beethoven's Ninth Symphony*.

SYMPHONY NO. 2
In D Major, Op. 73
FIRST PERFORMANCE: VIENNA, DECEMBER 30, 1877

Brahms was an inveterate walker. He liked to stuff his pockets full of candy and stroll to some outlying spot on the Worthersee, loveliest of South Austrian lakes, dispensing candy to children as he went along. The children were a bit afraid. To them his kindly gruffness and his harsh, North German accent were signals for retreat.

But even so, Brahms liked to talk to them, when they would talk. He also liked to sit alone on some deserted bench—watching the gently lapping waters of the lake, the sky, the birds, the foliage, the squirrels in the trees— feeling at peace with the entire world and letting himself slip into a mood of peaceful musing.

"So many melodies fly about here," he later wrote on the subject of his Second Symphony on which he was then working, "that one must be wary not to step on them."

This Second Symphony, composed barely a year after the epic First, is an idyll of tender, pastoral serenity and flowing, gentle melody.

GUIDE TO LISTENING

First Movement: A dusky melody in the French horn starts this movement quietly on its way. The atmosphere is one of gentle contemplation, and in this mood the music continues to unfold. Drifting loftily, it progresses, finally immersing us, as Hanslick so well put it "in a clear wave of melody upon which we rest, swayed and refreshed."

Second Movement: There are accents of gloom in the broadly exalted musical speech of the second movement. Yet, if this be tragedy, it never breaks over our heads. We are here face to face with Brahms the philosopher, mature and meditative.

Third Movement: Sunny is the atmosphere

of this movement, built upon a single theme
which we hear voiced by oboe, clarinets, and
bassoons with 'cello accompaniment.

Fourth Movement: This movement has been
said to have Mozartian blood in its veins. It
is contagious in its care-free gayety, its spunk,
its rollicking good humor, its closing accents
of exhilaration.

CONCERTO (VIOLIN AND ORCHESTRA)
In D Major, Op. 77
FIRST PERFORMANCE: LEIPZIG, JANUARY 1, 1879

Shortly after the warm public reception
accorded to his Second Symphony, Brahms
decided that he needed a vacation and was
soon on a southbound train. Italy, where he
traveled, put him in the best of spirits. Its
natural beauty, its people, its sunshine, its
works of art delighted him, and he carried
over into his Violin Concerto some of this
warmth, this glow, this animation which he
had experienced during the trip.

GUIDE TO LISTENING

First Movement: A long and fluid orchestral
introduction (in which all of the sombre-
hued instruments—violas, 'cellos, bassoons—

intone the principal theme) shifts abruptly
to a sullen, angry mood. The solo instrument now enters, and the music quickly gains
in intensity, subsides to a song-like melody,
then rises again to a vigorous end.

Second Movement: A charming, pastoral melody voiced by the oboe is followed by the
entry of the solo instrument which embroiders
the melody in a quiet, meditative way.

Third Movement: In sharp contrast to the
preceding movement is this brilliant music
in which melodies of Hungarian cast lead
with fervor to a triumphant climax. (Brahms'
fondness for Hungarian style finales is probably traceable to his close association with
the Hungarian violinist Remenyi with whom
he went on a concert tour when twenty.)

ACADEMIC FESTIVAL OVERTURE
Op. 80
FIRST PERFORMANCE: BRESLAU, JANUARY 4, 1881

In 1876 Cambridge University notified
Brahms that it wanted to confer on him an
honorary doctor's degree. At first overjoyed,
Brahms curtly refused when he learned that
the University required him to make a personal appearance at Cambridge in order to
receive the degree. This he later attributed

to what he termed his "great distaste for concerts and other disturbances." Actually, his refusal was motivated by his fear of the sea—a dread so childishly unreasonable that he would not willingly have crossed the English Channel even if the Crown of England were awaiting him on the other side.

However, when a few years later the University of Breslau conferred on him a Doctorate of Philosophy, Brahms not only accepted the honor but responded by composing an overture to commemorate the occasion— his *Academic Festival Overture.*

GUIDE TO LISTENING

The rollicking overture is a fantasy ingeniously built on four German college songs.

TRAGIC OVERTURE
Op. 81
FIRST PERFORMANCE: VIENNA 1880 (OR BRESLAU, JANUARY 4, 1881)

Brahms had his peculiarities—as a musician no less than as a man. One was his fondness for introducing in his scores a sort of greeting to the older masters (by briefly echoing some of these masters' music). Another was his habit of producing compositions of similar type in pairs—very different yet somehow complementary—among others, his First and Second Symphonies, and his *Academic Festival* and *Tragic Overtures*.

This latter overture, believed to have been written originally as incidental music for Goethe's *Faust,* was later recast by the composer as an independent orchestral work.

GUIDE TO LISTENING

The work is characterized by a certain ominous and decorous reserve, giving at first the effect of a hush of expectation. As the Viennese critic, Edward Hanslick, remarks: Brahms has taken as his subject "the universal, constant, fundamental emotion of tragedy." Yet, as Lawrence Gilman pointedly retorts: "Tragic is scarcely the word for a work which, while realizing all the sadness of life, yet sends the hearer away all the stronger for having heard it."

CONCERTO (PIANO AND ORCHESTRA) NO. 2

In B-Flat Major, Op. 83

FIRST PERFORMANCE: BUDAPEST, NOVEMBER 9, 1881

This Concerto, like its famous predecessor for the violin, bears the stamp of what Brahms called "the miracle of Southern Spring turning to summer"; for it was sketched in 1878, on the heels of an exhilarating trip to Italy. Brahms completed the work three years later—and, incidentally, at that time also grew his famous beard, because, as he put it, "a smooth chin makes people mistake you either for an actor or a priest."

But the public's reception of the work was lukewarm, and Franz Liszt to whom Brahms had sent the manuscript wrote back: "Frankly speaking, at first reading, this work seemed to me a bit gray in tone."

It took the Concerto a long time to push its way to the front.

GUIDE TO LISTENING

First Movement: Peacefully, the French horn announces a limpid, question-like melodic phrase and is answered softly by the orchestra. The piano, already heard accompanying the horn, now enters with vibrant intensity, and soon the entire orchestra takes up the main theme, of which the initial horn passage was but a fragment.

Second Movement: Impetuous and heaving, this opening draws a shadow across our tonal horizon which, until now, was bathed in the memory of the first movement's springlike lyricism.

Third Movement: A melody in the 'cello,

song-like, gravely amorous, opens the movement. A great peace settles on us and envelops us on all sides. Following some rhapsodizing by the piano, the song-like melody returns, and the music seems to drift away like a quiet end of evening on some distant hills on the misty horizon.

Fourth Movement: A lightness of mood that is charmingly carefree, with a dash of Hungarian flavor and a whimsical digression here and there—we can almost see the glint in Brahms' eye—carries us along to a brightly dazzling end.

SYMPHONY NO. 3
In F Major, Op. 90
FIRST PERFORMANCE: VIENNA, DECEMBER 2, 1883

In the year 1883, the year of Wagner's death, Brahms, with the completion of his Third Symphony, reached his full stature as a symphonist. With this symphony, too, at fifty-one, he experienced at last the gratification of prompt financial return, for the publication of the work in 1884 netted him an initial fee of nine thousand dollars.

Many writers have sought the inner meaning of Brahms' Third Symphony, but no one else perhaps has said so much in so few words as the Viennese critic Hanslick in whose opinion the work differs from the "poignant song of Fate" characterizing the First Symphony, no less than from the "joyful Idyl," characteristic of the Second, in that "its fundamental note is proud strength that rejoices in deeds."

GUIDE TO LISTENING

First Movement: The upper notes of the three chords that open this movement constitute a "motto" which reappears throughout the Symphony. Soon the first theme—sweeping and slowly growing in ardor—makes its appearance. A second, pastoral-like theme provides a brief respite, but the music soon rises again in intensity, slackens in pace, and ends in a mood of luminous calm.

Second Movement: Restrained and lovely is this movement, bespeaking a tranquility not to be found in a younger Brahms. It is the tranquility of advancing years, mellowed by a realization of things accomplished; ripened, too, by a philosophical detachment from youth's turbulent cares.

Third Movement: This movement has a folk song—one is almost tempted to say, a childlike—simplicity whose appeal is immediate. Softly brooding is this music, glowing with gentle wistfulness.

Fourth Movement: After a few deeply menacing bars, a turbulent note is struck. Then the music surges, rapidly plunging us into a mood of passionate conflict. Aggressively the music unfolds, by turns savage and solemn, but it finally subsides to a great peacefulness which envelops us on all sides.

SYMPHONY NO. 4
In E Minor, Op. 98
FIRST PERFORMANCE: MEININGEN, OCTOBER 25, 1885

By 1884, at the time of the writing of his Fourth Symphony, Brahms was already fairly well off. He would have been rich, had he been less scrupulous in his work and a little more gifted in the art of self-advertising. "The hard thing," he once remarked, "is not to compose, but to let the superfluous notes fall under the table." Practicing what he preached and ignoring his anxious publishers, he ruthlessly destroyed compositions that failed to measure up to his standards—dozens of string quartets, hundreds of songs.

Although Brahms labored especially hard on his Fourth Symphony, and although the work rose from the start to a place of high esteem among musicians, it was slow to gain public favor. Only recently can it be said

[59]

to have finally escaped its enforced obscurity, aligning itself in popularity with its three great sister symphonies.

GUIDE TO LISTENING

First Movement: Flowing, lyrical, and somehow intensely invigorating, is the first melody with which the work opens. It unfolds with great forcefulness—yet its power never thrusts itself ostentatiously on the listener—and it ends on a note of quiet self-confidence.

Elisabet von Herzogenberg, Brahms' devoted friend who was the first to see the Symphony in manuscript, wrote to the composer, giving him her first impressions of the work. She said:

Second Movement: "The Andante has the distinction which you only could give it . . . How freely flowing . . . how exquisite in its melodiousness it all is . . . like pressing through exquisite scenery at sunset—when the colors deepen and the crimson turns to purple."

Third Movement: "After this feast," (the second movement) "I felt I needed a breathing spell to adjust to the irresistible, rough humor of the scherzo; but soon I surrendered heart and soul to its great gayety and impetus—so playful, so frivolous, yet so lovely. . . ."

Fourth Movement: "As for the last movement," (a stately yet very simple theme followed by its repetition in thirty-one successive variations) "do you mind if I nominate this as my favorite—at least, for the time being. The theme itself fascinates me, and the fascination increases as I hear it through its various stages—first low, then high, or else deftly hidden somewhere in the middle; and, most wonderful of all . . . in its trombone repetition in the golden key of E major. . . . One need, thank Heaven, not be a musician to come under its spell."

Violin

John Alden Carpenter

Born 1876 at Park Ridge, Illinois, of Pilgrim ancestry. Was introduced to music early by his mother. After graduating from Harvard entered family business in Chicago (cordage distributors) where he became a major executive. Though practicing music as an avocation, became an accomplished composer writing in an agreeable melodic idiom. Is best known for his suite *Adventures in a Perambulator* and his jazz ballet *Skyscrapers*.

ADVENTURES IN A PERAMBULATOR
Suite for Orchestra
FIRST PERFORMANCE: CHICAGO, MARCH 19, 1915

Imagine the sensations—keen yet out of focus—of an infant taken for an outing by his nurse—an infant wheeled around in a perambulator and confronted for the first time in his life by such amazing realities as a Policeman (who flirts with the Nurse) ; a

Hurdy Gurdy (which produces most insidious noises) ; a Lake (where the land comes to an end) ; and Dogs (which laugh, fight, and play) .

On this captivating idea John Alden Carpenter has built his amusing suite.

GUIDE TO LISTENING

A short introduction acquaints us with the principal characters of the piece.

"And now, we're off—my Nurse's steps resounding firmly behind." Soon the Policeman makes a pompous appearance (you hear his measured tread) , and his voice (solo bassoon) mingles with that of the Nurse (violins) . After a short interlude, familiar strains of the Hurdy Gurdy float past us on the breeze. We catch snatches of *Alexander's Rag Time Band.* Fainter and fainter grows the Hurdy Gurdy. After a pause, the Nurse wheels me away. We now hear the quiet rippling of a Lake (flute), the occasional splash of a wave (strings and French horns) . The Nurse sits down on a bench. Nearby, dogs bark and frolic, start a game of *Follow the Leader.*

Homeward bound, at last. "My mind grows numb. My cup is full. I have a sudden conviction that it is well I am not alone. That firm step behind reassures me." Thinking of my mother I drop off to sleep.

Frédéric Chopin

BORN 1810 AT ZELAZOWA WOLA in Poland—
his father a Frenchman who taught French
to the well-to-do; his mother, the daughter
of an impoverished Polish nobleman.
Frédéric, the second of four children, displayed such a remarkable aptitude for the
piano that at eight, after a concert at Warsaw, he was hailed locally as a second Mozart.
At fifteen, already a composer, he saw his
music in print. At twenty-one, he journeyed
to Paris where he was acclaimed and where
he soon acquired more wealthy young women,
as piano students, than he could handle.
Never very strong physically, in 1836 he found
his health failing but continued feverishly
to compose for another ten years until overcome by his malady—consumption. Died
1849 (aged 39) in Paris and is remembered
as the greatest of all composers of music for
the piano.

Chopin's music is permeated with romantic intimacy. Whether nostalgic or passionately heroic, its appeal remains essentially feminine; its message that of a sensitive poet gifted with a melodic eloquence probably unsurpassed.

CONCERTO (PIANO AND ORCHESTRA) NO. 1
In E Minor, Op. 11
FIRST PERFORMANCE: WARSAW, OCTOBER 11, 1830

Throughout his brief life Chopin remained in a tightly sealed little world of his own. High strung and of delicate sensibilities, he loathed anything gross or uncouth; but he was also a little too obviously fond of elegance in clothes, refinement in manners, and breeding in women not to pass for a snob—which he was—for he mixed best with aristocrats whose social outlook strengthened his undemocratic bias acquired early in youth.

Once, commenting on a street demonstration in Paris, he wrote to a friend: "I can scarcely describe the unpleasant impression made on me by the horrible shouting of these rioters and the sight of the rebellious mob." As it turned out, it was a demonstration in honor of Poland which he had mistaken for a revolutionary outbreak.

Frédéric Chopin

Indeed, this shy, delicately built, irresolute, tortured, morbidly sensitive Pole shrank from the least contact with the people; and, strangely enough, for his contacts in Paris were wide, he cared naught for any of the other arts. Of Victor Hugo, one of the few French authors he had sampled, Chopin said: "He is too coarse and violent."

This distrust and dislike of anything too bold or too realistic, which was so important an element of Chopin's make-up as a man, finds its reflection in Chopin the musician. Contrary to popular opinion, Chopin was not the sentimentalist which some overzealous performers of his music have made him out to be. Essentially, though, he was a miniaturist, aware of his limitations, aware also of his great potentialities, remarkably wise for his age and temperament in sticking to the field in which his particular gifts made him unique—composition for the piano.

Chopin wrote almost exclusively for that instrument. Yet, since in his day, to be taken seriously, a composer had to express himself in broader terms, Chopin complied by writing two concertos for piano and orchestra.

GUIDE TO LISTENING

First Movement: The work starts off resolutely. Before long, the piano enters—at first playing alone, then together with the orchestra, as it develops the first theme. The music increases in vigor, subsides momentarily in a flowing, lyrical passage, then again becomes agitated, and, after several wistfully lovely interludes, closes on a vigorous chord. *Second Movement:* Begins with a brooding passage in the strings, which serves to introduce the chief theme, played with elusive sadness by the piano. In this mood, which is both tender and serene, the music—called a romance—progresses to its quietly poetic end.

Third Movement: This movement is probably the most ingratiating of the three, vivacious and playful, and at the same time somehow more personal in its appeal—sparkling in its melodiousness, brilliant in its energetic close.

CONCERTO (PIANO AND ORCHESTRA) NO. 2

In F Minor, Op. 21

FIRST PERFORMANCE: WARSAW, MARCH 17, 1830

Young Chopin fell in love in 1829 with a young girl, Constantia Gladkowska, a student at the Warsaw Conservatory, whom he had not the nerve to approach, but of whom he wrote: "I venerate her faithfully and truly. . . . It was with thoughts of this lovely creature that I composed the Adagio of my new Concerto. . . ." (He was presumably referring to the second movement of his F minor Concerto.)

This concerto, though called No. 2, was actually the first to be composed and second only in order of publication. Many, though, consider it superior—"more human" says Huneker—to the E minor work.

GUIDE TO LISTENING

First Movement: The work opens in the orchestra with an extensive passage of very martial demeanor. Finally, as if tired of waiting, the piano makes a dramatic appearance. There follow some intensely brilliant passages which subside to a mood of romantic brooding.

Second Movement: Is slow and rhapsodic almost to the point of exaltation. About half way through, its typically Chopinesque loveliness is suddenly dissipated. Stridently, the piano announces this change, and the music grows increasingly agitated, but it returns before closing to its original rhapsodic mood.

Third Movement: Is lively, mazurka-like rhythmically, and extremely brilliant pianistically.

Claude Debussy

Born 1862 at Saint-Germain near Paris, the son of a china shop merchant. Entered the Paris Conservatory at eleven where, already in revolt against traditional harmony, he proved himself something of a problem. After collecting several minor prizes, at twenty-two won the famous Prix de Rome which took him to Italy. In subsequent years, with headquarters in Paris, devoted himself to conducting, musical criticism, and the writing of works which, regarded at first as musical nightmares, earned him reputation, fame, immortality. Died of cancer 1918 (aged 56) in Paris.

The music of Claude Debussy is sensitive, moody, and has to be met more than half-way if it is to be wooed. Only to the sympathetic listener is it ready to yield; only such a listener will it reward by transporting him into regions mysterious where he may dwell in the kingdom of nebulous fancy, breathing

Claude Debussy

a rarified atmosphere of shimmering sound.
Dreamy yet strangely vivid is this music;
elusive but very personal and very intimate,
is its appeal.

(For other works by Debussy, see *Recommended Recordings.*)

PRELUDE TO THE AFTERNOON
OF A FAUN

FIRST PERFORMANCE: PARIS, DECEMBER 22, 1894

When Rimsky-Korsakoff heard Debussy's
operatic landmark, *Pélleas and Mélisande,* he
was moved to remark: "I will have nothing
more to do with this music lest I should un-
happily develop a liking for it." Rimsky
does not record his impressions of *The Afternoon of a Faun* (which was composed the
same year that the opera was begun) and it
is just possible that the aging Russian never
heard it; but from others we gather the nature of most people's reaction to this now
famous piece.

Today we take Debussy so much for granted
that we find it hard to believe the testimony
of one present at the initial performance of
The Afternoon of a Faun; for this eyewitness
reports being "struck with consternation at
the hisses of the public." On second thought,

[70]

though, this reaction appears less surprising. Debussy had dared to be different. He had fashioned an eerie, highly evocative tone painting, unlike anything heretofore experienced in music. No wonder the music-loving public and critics found themselves temporarily in a state of confusion verging on consternation!

Debussy had originally intended writing this musical setting of Mallarmé's poem in three parts: a Prelude, an Interlude, and a Finale—but only the Prelude was finished in time for the concert, and Debussy never completed the other two parts.

GUIDE TO LISTENING

A young faun's awakening in the forest is signalized by a gravely sensuous melody announced by the flute. Transparent threads of sound are woven into a languid, exquisitely suggestive texture as the faun bends to pick up a golden-headed lily and tries to remember whether the visitation of beautiful nymphs, of which he is still so deliciously conscious, was a reality or a dream. But his brain is not equal to the effort. Vaguer and vaguer grows the memory, more and more alluring the soft grass at his feet; and so he curls up again under a tree, there to pursue the ecstasy of his vision in sleep.

NOCTURNES: NO. I, "CLOUDS"— NO. II, "FESTIVALS"—NO. III, "SIRENS"

FIRST PERFORMANCE: PARIS, (I & II) DECEMBER 9, 1900; (III) OCTOBER 27, 1901

"It is exactly at the moment when language is unable to voice the expression of the soul that the vocation of music is opened to us; if all that passes in us were capable of expression in words, I should write no more music."

These words, from the pen of Mendelssohn, might as well have been Debussy's. For if the Frenchman's artistic aim could be summed up in one sentence, it would be that he strove to express through music what could not be otherwise expressed. Or, stating it a bit differently, as W. H. Daly has done: "Any reasonably competent draughtsman can fill a drawing, to the point of intricacy, with exactly correct detail. To carry out the reverse process of omission, takes something of a genius."

Just such a genius was Debussy. His art, above all, was suggestive—an effort not to conjure for our benefit a photographic vision of clouds, or festivals, or sirens, but to make

us sense from contact with a few deftly arranged sound combinations the inner meaning of clouds and festivals and sirens; to
make us "get" their essential feeling as the
composer himself felt them to be.

This aim, of course, was not original with
Debussy. What was original, and highly unusual, was its realization. For Debussy
achieved his purpose not with the help of
conventional melody or any known device of
musical architecture, but through massed
bodies of tone, always shifting, strangely
elusive, completely lacking in any formal design.

The production of these orchestral Nocturnes marked Debussy's first unqualified
public success. The explanatory notes quoted
below are the composer's.

GUIDE TO LISTENING

Clouds: ". . . pictures the unchanging aspect
of the sky and the slow, solemn motion of
clouds, fading away in grey tints lightly
touched with white."

Festivals: ". . . renders the restless, dancing
rhythm of the atmosphere, interspersed with
sudden flashes of light." A mysterious fanfare by the trumpets introduces a procession
"which passes through the aerial revelry and
becomes merged with it."

Sirens: ". . . depicts the sea with its perpetual rhythm; the mysterious song of passing sirens is heard amid the waves silvered by the moonlight." (This piece is the longest of the three and is extremely difficult in its wordless women's chorus in which the voices are treated as instruments.)

LA MER
Three Symphonic Sketches
FIRST PERFORMANCE: PARIS, OCTOBER 15, 1905

La Mer, it seems clear, is Debussy's chef-d'œuvre—a towering work which stands up well when placed alongside the various other masterpieces of music. In it Debussy, who was essentially a miniaturist, for once was able to project his message onto a large canvas with a strength and directness perfectly matched to his subject.

La Mer, which presents three different aspects of the sea, elicited sharp complaints from the critics when first performed. One wrote that the work made him "neither hear, nor see, nor feel the sea." Another said it did not measure up to the composer's earlier works. The majority seem to have agreed in considering themselves let down by the absence in the piece of that "nebulous" quality which they had come to regard as the distinguishing mark of Debussy's music.

In detecting this lack the critics were right. They were wrong in considering it a weakness. For through the years, more and more people have come to cherish this musical impression of the sea—a monument alike to Nature and to the insignificance of man.

GUIDE TO LISTENING

From Dawn till Noon on the Sea: There is a mysterious quality in the opening bars of the music. Muted trumpet and English horn sound the chief theme, and, as they do so, the sea becomes more animated.

The Play of Waves: Pictures the sea now thoroughly awakened by the wind—its waves endlessly racing each other and tossing wet spray high in the air where it scatters in a thousand flakes of iridescent color.

Dialogue of the Wind and the Sea: Paints a stormier sea—a sea heaving, mysterious; its mood, sullen; its windswept surface angry with foam, rolling out of eye's reach; its voice conjuring immensities beyond man's grasp or power to control.

◇◇◇◇◇◇◇◇◇◇◇◇◇◇◇◇◇◇◇◇◇◇◇◇◇◇◇◇◇◇

Paul Dukas

BORN 1865 AT PARIS, France. Showed marked
ability while studying at the Paris Conservatory. Following graduation and two years
of military training, devoted himself to composition and musical criticism, becoming the
director of the Paris Conservatory in 1928.
Has written a number of works, notably the
opera *Ariane et Barbe Bleue* but is known
outside of France chiefly for his symphonic
scherzo *The Sorcerer's Apprentice*, an international favorite and a piece of genuine
originality. Died of heart disease in 1935
(aged 70) at Paris, France.

THE SORCERER'S APPRENTICE
Scherzo for Orchestra
FIRST PERFORMANCE: PARIS, MAY 18, 1897

The ballad by Goethe which inspired Paul
Dukas to compose this impish tonal anecdote

is based on a tale at least eighteen hundred years old. This tale concerns itself with the adventures of a magician's apprentice who, in his master's absence, tinkers with the machinery of the supernatural and almost comes to grief in the process.

GUIDE TO LISTENING

The opening harmonies—mysterious and a bit acrid—signalize the magician, about to depart. When he is gone, the apprentice tries his hand at the cabalistic craft. He invokes a secret formula. There is a resounding thump, and the broom begins to move from its corner.

The broom comes back with a pail of water, which it dumps on the floor—makes another, and yet another trip. Horrified, the apprentice tries to remember the latter part of the formula, to stop the broom—but it doesn't work. In desperation he seizes an ax and slits the broom in two. For an instant the broom is still—but now there are two brooms fetching water. Faster and faster they go, and the room is being flooded.

At this juncture the magician returns, dreadful blasts in the brass section of the orchestra signalizing his appearance. He quickly puts both the broom and the apprentice—in their places.

Antonin Dvořák

Born 1841 at nelahozeves in Bohemia, the son of an innkeeper. His playing of the violin as a child at his father's inn, and his early compositions, led him eventually to the Organ School in Prague. Graduating at eighteen, he joined a concert band with which he stayed for a number of years, marrying at thirty-two and winning the Austrian State Prize for composition the following year. Thereafter enjoyed a steadily growing recognition, as a result of which he journeyed nine times to England and once to America where he stayed for over three years. In 1902 became the head of the Prague Conservatory and a member of the Austrian Parliament. Died 1904 (aged 62) and is remembered as a great Czech folk composer, second only to Smetana.

Dvořák's music is high-spirited and virile, Not infrequently it can be whimsical or ardently poetic. Although it is distinctly Slavic in mood, it usually skirts the darker

aspects of the Slavic temperament. Though
it is always highly accomplished and polished, its chief charm lies in its forthrightness
which it derives from its link with Czech folk
music. (For other works by Dvořák see *Recommended Recordings*.)

SYMPHONY NO. 5
In E Minor, Op. 95 (*From the New World*)

FIRST PERFORMANCE: NEW YORK, DECEMBER 15,
1893

The idea of journeying to the U. S. A.—a
land musically still in the kindergarten stage
—and of braving a great stretch of ocean in
order to get there, held little appeal for the
continental Dvořák. But the salary he was
offered to head the National Conservatory in
New York—a salary fabulous in terms of his
native Bohemia—overcame his hesitations.
He came to America; and, once in the United
States, he quickly adapted himself to his new
environment.

There was much in the New World to fas-
cinate Dvořák; much to disturb him, too,
and baffle his nationalistic outlook. Among
other things he found it hard to understand
why native American composers looked so
persistently to Europe for their inspiration in-

stead of taking advantage of their own musical heritage, both Negro and Indian. "These beautiful and varied melodies," he kept repeating to his students in New York, "are the product of the soil. They are American, and composers must turn to them. . . . Only in this way can a musician express the true sentiment of the people. . . ."

With characteristic thoroughness, Dvořák undertook a study of Negro and Indian melodies. He then wrote several works. These he tried to compose in the spirit of what he regarded as native American music; and to these works he later pointed in illustration of what he meant by the influence on musical composition of a country's racial and national characteristics.

Of these American compositions of Dvořák's, the most famous is the symphony *From the New World*. The gusto of this work and its melodic and rhythmic charm have made it one of the most popular of all symphonies.

GUIDE TO LISTENING

First Movement: The work opens with a pensive, sighing passage, stated by the strings and repeated by the woodwinds. The orchestra now lunges ominously, and the first vehement theme, introduced by the French horns, soon makes its appearance. After a rousing climax, we hear the second theme—a melody believed to have been inspired by the Negro tune *Old Man Moses, He Sells His Roses* which it closely resembles.

Second Movement: After a brief but majestic and solemn introduction, the English horn ushers in a lovely melody, soon taken up by other instruments. A halo seems to hang over the music from this point on, for it unfolds in the tender yet passionate mood of a rhapsodic song, broken into once, but quickly resumed.

Third Movement: Is vital, barbaric in its beating rhythms, said to have grown out of Dvořák's study of the music of American Indians. Its vitality unabated, the music progresses, its second theme—which is more jovial—leading back to the original mood.

Fourth Movement: A brief introduction ushers in a militant proclamation by horns and trumpets, following which the music advances with tremendous gusto. We now hear echoes from the preceding movements, and the work finally reaches its thunderous climax.

Georges Enesco

BORN 1881 AT LIVENI, Rumania, the son of a well-to-do farmer. Began to play the violin at four and embarked, at seven, on a fruitful period of study, first at the Vienna, then at the Paris conservatories. During these years, in addition to acquiring a remarkable mastery of the violin—his first love—also became an accomplished pianist, 'cellist, and organist; later, a conductor of eminence and a composer of force and imagination—the founder of a Rumanian School of composition.

RUMANIAN RHAPSODY NO. 1
In A Major, Op. 11
FIRST PERFORMANCE: PARIS, FEBRUARY 1908

The story is told that Enesco, as a child of four, asked his father for a fiddle. Though startled by this request from so young a child, the elder Enesco complied. He brought

home a violin with three strings. To his
amazement, his precocious son registered
great displeasure, remarking after he had ex-
amined the instrument: "I asked for a violin,
not a plaything."

Soon after this incident, a real violin was
procured, and the youngster immediately
picked up and learned to embroider upon all
of the village tunes circulating in the neighboring countryside—tunes which he was later
to bring together in two Rumanian Rhap-
sodies, of which the first is the best known.

GUIDE TO LISTENING

The Rhapsody, which is a free improvisa-
tion on several Rumanian folk melodies, opens
with a very gypsy-like tune, suggested by
clarinet and oboe, and soon taken up in a
rousing statement by the entire orchestra. In
this light vein the music unfolds, in turn
rhapsodic and spirited, but mostly the latter,
right up to its rousing end.

Rumania, incidentally, is a Latin country
concerning whose music Enesco has said:
"Our music . . . is influenced not by the
neighboring Slav, but by the Indian and
Egyptian folk songs, introduced by the members of these remote races, now classed as
gypsies."

César Franck

BORN 1822 AT LIEGE, Belgium, the son of a
Flemish bank clerk. Showed talent for music
at an early age and was packed off on a concert tour as a pianist when barely eleven. At
fifteen, won several prizes at the Paris Conservatory. At twenty-six, married a French
actress and settled in Paris to a frugal and industrious life as organist and teacher, composing as time permitted. During his life received probably less official and public
recognition for his music than any other
ranking composer. Died in 1890 (aged 68)
at Paris, France, from pleurisy aggravated by
an accident in which he was knocked over
by a bus.

The music of César Franck is unique
through the quality of exalted brooding that
permeates it. Whether serene or troubled, it
moves on a lofty plane of pious, almost mystic contemplation, sometimes attaining an ecstatic character which is profoundly moving.

SYMPHONIC VARIATIONS
For Piano and Orchestra
FIRST PERFORMANCE: PARIS, MAY 1, 1885

It is told that César Franck once went to a
gathering of musicians where he was introduced to Bizet. During the brief conversation that followed, the composer of *Carmen*
is said to have expressed great surprise at
hearing that Franck, too, wrote music.

It undoubtedly would have surprised Bizet
even more if some voice from the future could
have whispered to him that this unpretentious
fellow with whom he was conversing—this
graying and wholly negligible little professor
of organ playing—would one day be regarded
as a great composer, and his *Symphonic Variations* as one of the most original and en-
gaging musical works of the period.

GUIDE TO LISTENING

The work opens with two adjoining melodies—the first vehement, aggressive, uttered
by the strings; the second melodious and sub-
missive, entrusted to the piano. On these
two melodies Franck lavishes his creative
fancy, fashioning and refashioning them in a
set of sparkling variations which transport us

through moods of lively joy and tender melancholy, of religious contemplation and full-blooded, tumultuous vitality.

SYMPHONY
In D Minor
FIRST PERFORMANCE: PARIS, FEBRUARY 17, 1889

César Franck's saving grace was his health and his amiable disposition, but his courage and patience must have often been strained to the breaking point. He had friends, mostly fellow musicians, who recognized his genius and did all they could to secure the performance of his works. But as the years rolled by, the public remained strangely indifferent, and so unaware of his activities as a composer was official France that when it finally decided to reward his services with a ribbon of the Legion of Honor, it designated the recipient as—"Professor of Organ."

It took him two long years to complete his Symphony, and César Franck—then in his sixties—labored hard. Since his days were taken up teaching and playing the organ, he worked on the symphony Sundays and holidays, and he worked every morning, rising promptly at five. Such is the story of this great musical work, a large part of which was produced before breakfast. Today it is one of the most frequently played of all symphonies, but the composer heard it publicly performed only once, and then mainly because his friends had the energy and perseverance to overcome all opposition—a hostility which extended even to the members of the orchestra.

GUIDE TO LISTENING

First Movement: A low, questioning phrase in the strings opens the Symphony. Immediately, the violins sing out an incisively eloquent answer. They dwell on it, as if reluctant to break off, but the question is repeated, again and again—calmly at first, then almost angrily and loudly by the entire string section of the orchestra. This musical material serves as a starting point. It is developed at length—now surging, now receding—lifting us more and more into regions which transcend the petty and the trivial in our lives.

Second Movement: After a short introduction the English horn sings out a peculiarly expressive and pensive melody, over an accompaniment of plucked strings. Presently the melody is picked up by the clarinet and French horn. After an extended development, there is a decided change to a brighter mood.

César Franck

Third Movement: This movement starts with
a jerk, and the opening melody, voiced at
first by the 'cellos and bassoons, gains in
vehemence as it unfolds. Exultantly the
violins pick it up. Now the music grows
quieter, but it mounts quickly again. Carried
along by the music we seem to struggle, torn
between the powers of light and the forces of
darkness. At last, as the movement reaches
its great climax of frenzied ecstasy, we are
made to feel that light has triumphed over
darkness, that for a brief instant we have
been admitted to a vision of our soul's ulti-
mate destiny.

French Horn

George Gershwin

Born 1898 in Brooklyn, New York. His father kept the family constantly on the go, for he switched from the running of restaurants to the management of Turkish baths, etc., etc. At thirteen, young Gershwin settled down to the serious study of the piano, for he loved music. This led to his employment by a music firm in New York. Before long he had composed some songs and sold them—to another firm. Gradually he built a reputation as a song writer and, in 1919, he was given an opportunity to write a whole show. In 1924, with the playing of *The Rhapsody in Blue,* he became famous, but his promising career was prematurely ended in 1937 when he died (aged 38) of a brain tumor in Hollywood.

Gershwin's music has the driving, nervous energy and excitement of the jazz age. Yet it is distinguishable from all other jazz in that it bears the stamp of a sensitive musical

personality sufficiently unique to reach beyond the world of Broadway's Tin Pan Alley.

CONCERTO (PIANO AND ORCHESTRA)
In F Major

FIRST PERFORMANCE: NEW YORK, DECEMBER 3, 1925

Gershwin's *Rhapsody in Blue* was written
in a little over three weeks at the instigation
of Paul Whiteman who had always wanted
to perform jazz in the concert hall but had
never before found any jazz music sufficiently enduring for the purpose. The
Rhapsody was a hit. It brought Gershwin
a commission from the New York Symphony
Society. Delighted, the young composer produced his Piano Concerto in F, and in this
work for the first time he did his own scoring
for the orchestra.

GUIDE TO LISTENING

First Movement: The work opens with a
characteristic jazz rhythm, established by the
kettledrums, the principal theme soon announced by the bassoon. The piano now
enters with the broader and more restrained
second theme which leads to an extensive
and often exciting development.

Second Movement: Is melancholy, permeated with the atmosphere of the old Negro South.

Third Movement: Is short, furiously nervous, driven by its typically Gershwin rhythms.

Piano

Michael Glinka

Born 1804 at Novoprasskoye in Southwest Russia, the son of a nobleman. As a child showed great interest in music, which he later cultivated as an amateur. Following completion of his studies, became a civil employee of the Government but resigned at twenty-six to devote himself to music. After a trip to Italy wrote the national Russian opera *Life for the Tsar* which, chiefly because of its patriotic character, met with great success. Subsequent works, of which the best known is the orchestra fantasia *Kamarinskaya,* were less favorably received, but through Glinka's pioneering efforts the way was cleared for the rise of a vigorous school of Russian national composers including Moussorgsky, Borodin, Rimsky-Korsakoff and others. Died 1857 (aged 53) at Berlin, Germany. Although not a major composer himself, is remembered as the "Prophet-Patriarch" of Russian music.

OVERTURE TO "RUSSLAN AND LUDMILLA"

FIRST PERFORMANCE: ST. PETERSBURG, DECEMBER
10, 1842

Glinka's appearance was of epoch-making
significance to the history of Russian art.
Because he spent his childhood years in rural
Russia, and because of his extreme sensitivity
to music, Glinka early developed a love for
the folk songs and dances of his homeland.
When he grew up, he decided that Russian
music, to be worthy of the name, should de-
rive its inspiration from these native melodies instead of trying, rather left-handedly,
to pattern itself after Italian models.

He therefore undertook the job of recast-
ing the primitive speech of the Russian folk
song into a polished art-idiom, thereby in-
curring opposition and sneers at what was
called "this music for coachmen." But
Glinka went right ahead. Though he did
not produce much himself, he succeeded in
setting the pace for practically all subsequent
Russian music.

Russlan and Ludmilla—Glinka's second
opera—is laid in pagan Russia and deals
with the tribulations of the Princess Lud-

Michael Glinka

milla who, kidnapped by the magician Chernomor, is finally rescued by the favorite of her three suitors, Russlan, whom she weds.

GUIDE TO LISTENING

The music of the Overture bursts forth impetuously in a Russian folk dance which is the chief theme of the piece. Other, equally zestful melodies, drawn from various parts of the opera, are heard as the music progresses.

Bassoon

Edvard Grieg

BORN 1843 AT BERGEN, Norway, the son of the British consul in that city (his great-grand-father was a Scotchman). As a youth studied music in Leipzig, Germany, where he had Arthur Sullivan (Gilbert & Sullivan) as a fellow student. A meeting with Richard Nordraak, first nationalist composer of Norway, fired his imagination—he was then twenty-one—and led to the development of his characteristic style. At twenty-four became a conductor and teacher in Norway's capital and thereafter rose steadily in prestige. Died 1907 (aged 64) at Bergen, the first Scandinavian composer to reach a world-wide audience.

Grieg's music derives its inspiration from the folk songs of Norway and has a Norse ring about it—a quality of rugged, heroic nobility which calls forth visions of that country's steep mountains, pine forests, and fjords.

Edvard Grieg

CONCERTO (PIANO AND ORCHESTRA)
In A Minor, Op. 16
FIRST PERFORMANCE: LEIPZIG: FEBRUARY 1872

In Grieg's romantic, spirited melodiousness
Tchaikowsky sensed a kindred spirit; and,
not unnaturally, he used superlatives in praise
of the Concerto: "What charm! What
warmth and passion! What teeming vitality . . . originality and beauty. . . ."

Today Grieg's Concerto excites us less. It
has been heard too often, played to death—
and it has aged, a fact reflected in its vir-
tual disappearance from the repertoire of
most ranking pianists. It is only fair to add
that *we* have changed, not the Concerto. Its
youthful charm, its freshness and its vigor
are still there.

GUIDE TO LISTENING

First Movement: An ominous drum roll, increasing in volume, bursts forth in a furious
proclamation by the piano, leading directly
to the statement by the woodwinds of the
pervasive first theme. From this point the
music unfolds with increasing zest and culminates in a brilliant passage for the solo
instrument.

Second Movement: Is sad, permeated with the pale glow of a northern twilight.

Third Movement: Starts off vigorously and exuberantly. When the tumult subsides, we hear a gently glowing melody, very characteristic of Grieg. This is just a passing interlude, for the original vitality reasserts itself, and the music progresses to a smashing climax.

Cello

Charles Tomlinson Griffes

BORN 1884 AT ELMIRA, New York, the son of
a business man. Studied in local school and,
while a youth, went to Germany to study
piano and composition. At twenty-three returned to New York, obtaining a teaching
position in a school at Tarrytown, N. Y.
Thereafter lived inconspicuously, teaching
and working on his music. Toward the end
of his life began to be watched by the dis-
cerning few in music who perceived in him
the makings of perhaps a major native composer. Died of pneumonia 1920 (aged 36) in
New York, leaving only a few works, of
which the most important is the symphonic
poem *The Pleasure Dome of Kubla Khan.*

THE WHITE PEACOCK

Op. 7, Originally One of *Four Roman
Sketches* for the Piano

FIRST PERFORMANCE NEW YORK, JUNE, 1919

Although brought up as a Baptist in a

conventional American family, Griffes early developed an intense interest in the Far East. One of his favorite authors was Lafcadio Hearn, a kindred spirit in literature, and it was after he had saturated himself with Hearn, that young Griffes began to absorb all of the literature he could find on Persia, Hindustan, Japan, and China.

Evidence of this intense interest soon made itself felt in his work. For though Griffes' music impresses one on first hearing by its resemblance to Debussy, the sympathetic listener soon discerns in it something else as well. In *The White Peacock*, Griffes was inspired by a poem of William Sharp.

GUIDE TO LISTENING

The music paints a garden on which a tropical sun beats relentlessly. This garden is rich in blooming magnolia, honey flowers, multicolored poppies, and pomegranate; and in it, "cream white and soft" struts a white peacock.

A languorous melody paints the beauty of the vain creature as it moves through the garden. Glistening with a subdued glow, strange chords flow one into the other, picturing the lush growth and vivid colors of the garden, the oppressive heat, the gorgeous plumage of the fowl.

George Frederick Handel

BORN 1685 AT HALLE, Germany, the son of a
barber in the service of a nobleman. Though
greatly gifted for music, studied law at the
University of Halle because of his father's
opposition to an artistic career. After his
father's death, joined a Hamburg orchestra
as violinist. At twenty-one, already a composer, went to Italy where the performance
of his music brought him fame and influential friends. With this success behind him,
returned to Germany as court composer in
Hanover. The following year went to England where his triumphs were even greater
than in Italy, and where he eventually became naturalized as a British subject. Losing
but recouping his fortunes several times,
finally went blind in 1752, but remained
active, playing the organ and conducting
until 1759 when he died (aged 74) in London. Was buried at Westminster Abbey and

is remembered as one of the greatest composers of all time.

"WATER MUSIC"

The *Water Music* was composed by Handel for a party held to entertain George I, then King of England. According to the report, the King, his entourage, and many guests boarded the royal barge one late afternoon in mid-July, 1717 and traveled up the Thames enjoying the scenery and listening to the *Water Music* which was played by fifty musicians occupying another barge.

It is from this incident that the name "Water Music" derives; and the King is said to have been so delighted with it that he ordered the music repeated once before and again after supper.

GUIDE TO LISTENING

The *Water Music* consists of twenty jovial airs, dance tunes, bourrées, hornpipes, etc., loosely joined in a kind of serenade. It is seldom performed in its entirety. Usually the music is played in the form of a suite consisting of five or six numbers drawn from the score.

Franz Joseph Haydn

BORN 1732 AT ROHRAU near Vienna, of Croatian peasant stock. The second of twelve children, Joseph, at five, went to live with a relative who taught him music but neglected to feed him properly. At eight the emaciated lad became a choir boy in Vienna. There, some years later, he began earning a precarious livelihood teaching and accompanying, meantime writing his first string quartet at twenty-three, and his first symphony at twenty-seven. Shortly thereafter, he found employment as musical director in the household of Prince Esterhazy, most powerful nobleman in the country. Remained in his castle for thirty years, composing, among other things, five masses, eleven operas, forty quartets, sixty symphonies, and becoming famous throughout Europe in the process. At fifty-eight went to England. Returning to Austria, lived quietly there until 1809 when he died (aged 77) in Vienna.

The music of Haydn has an earthy fresh-

ness and a verve utterly uninhibited, straight
from both the heart and the soil. It is unflagging in its imaginativeness and is very
much alive even today in its bubbling, rustic
optimism. (For other works by Haydn see
Recommended Recordings.)

SYMPHONY NO. 94
In G Major (*Surprise*)
FIRST PERFORMANCE: LONDON, MARCH 23, 1792

As a man, Haydn's most outstanding characteristic was his adaptability. Instead of
fretting away emotion and energy, he seems
to have possessed the valuable capacity of
overlooking the unpleasant side of any situation so long as he could extract from it some
good to himself as an artist. He had the
tenacity to stick to his chosen course; the patience to wait for an opening, when blocked.
In this he was greatly aided by the possession
of still another trait—a rare native good humor which expressed itself in his habit of
chuckling at the world, himself included; of
enjoying simple things; of living meanwhile as
fully as possible. This quality of good cheer
—strongly in evidence in this, most popular
of his symphonies—runs like a rippling stream
through most of Haydn's music.

Now it has been said that to stress this

particular quality of Haydn's music is to do
the composer an injustice since he also had
weightier, more urgently pertinent things
to say. To this it may be answered that so
far as weightier things are concerned, we
have Beethoven, Brahms, Sibelius, and others,
all of them weightier, more urgently pertinent than Haydn. But so far as brightness is
concerned—exhilarating, contagious, straight-
from-the-heart brightness—search as we may,
we can find no one to equal him.

GUIDE TO LISTENING

First Movement: The opening is slow, and
it has a genial formality about it, but soon a
melody typically Haydnesque in its playful
vivacity monopolizes the scene. Thereafter
the music unfolds with growing verve to a
spirited end.

Second Movement: Opens quietly, marching
along with disarming simplicity. The affable
melody is repeated, very softly, but after the
repetition there is a crashing chord (allegedly
intended by Haydn "to make the ladies sit
up" and responsible for the Symphony's
nickname *Surprise*). There follow four variations on the principal theme, bringing the
movement to a quiet close.

Third Movement: Is a minuet. It is brief,
charmingly unaffected, and its lilting rhythms

are the more ingratiating for all their naive, thoroughly eighteenth century flavor.

Fourth Movement: Gives us Haydn at his happiest. The grace and the sprightliness, the total lack of pretense and freshness of the music are well nigh irresistible. To a twentieth century audience, bowed down with sophisticated worry, it carries a measure of relief and satisfaction difficult to express in words.

SYMPHONY NO. 101
In D Major (*The Clock*)
FIRST PERFORMANCE: LONDON, MAY, 1794

In 1790, at the invitation of the violinist-impressario, Salomon, Haydn journeyed to London where he remained, off and on, about three years, writing seven hundred sixty-eight pages of new music and having a gloriously good time.

This music, embracing the twelve so-called *Salomon Symphonies*—among them the *Surprise, Clock,* and *London* symphonies—evoked, when performed, such enthusiasm from the usually placid British audiences that Haydn found himself lionized—dined, wined, loved, and even painted, the latter not without recrimination since the fifty-nine-year-old composer resented wasting perfectly good hours "just sitting."

Apparently the good time Haydn was having, far from impeding his creative vigor, stimulated it, and also deepened and broadened it, for these twelve symphonies produced in England are rated as Haydn's best.

GUIDE TO LISTENING

First Movement: The introductory passage is slow and hesitant, with a note of foreboding in its sustained tonal background. This shadowy mood persists for some time. It is abruptly dissipated by a swift melody which is, in fact, the chief theme of the movement. The music thereupon grows more and more animated, but the troubled mood is still somehow present in it to the very end.

Second Movement: From this movement the Symphony derives its name, for in it, from the start, bassoons and plucked strings are heard in what has been likened to an imitation of the ticking of a clock. Above this run several beautiful melodies, but the ticking is heard throughout most of the movement.

Third Movement: This is a robust minuet —a bit formal, a bit decorous, and very suggestive of a dance of courtiers and their ladies on the neatly trimmed lawn of a palace garden.

Fourth Movement: Animated and vital is this finale with its spirited exchanges between various instruments, moving right along to a brilliant end.

SYMPHONY NO. 104
In D Major (*London*)
FIRST PERFORMANCE: LONDON, MAY 4, 1795

Though Haydn did not actually invent the structure on which the symphony is based (*see C. P. E. Bach on page 3*) he did enlarge its scope and otherwise develop it. Because of this he has been called the "Father of the Symphony" (also of the Quartet). And because Haydn thus cleared the path for Beethoven, we not unnaturally find a certain resemblance between the compositions which Haydn wrote toward the end of his career and those Beethoven wrote when he was starting out.

This *London Symphony*—the last of Haydn's one hundred and four symphonies—bears out the point. For in emotional depth and in dramatic power it clearly foreshadows Beethoven.

GUIDE TO LISTENING
First Movement: The Symp
a broad, heroic proclamation,

hushed mysteriousness in the strings. Again
the proclamation is heard, and again the
veiled voices of the strings murmur the answer. After yet another repetition, the music
seems to spread out with sudden vitality,
moving with practically undiminished vigor
and dramatic intensity to the very end.

Second Movement: Is slow, rhapsodic, glowing with restrained passion. It is probably
the most mature music that Haydn ever
wrote, for it probes deeply, revealing a
breadth of vision and expression usually
linked with Beethoven's, rather than with
Haydn's, name.

Third Movement: Is a minuet, but—and note
this—it is not just another sprightly dance
tune such as Haydn turned out by the hundred. For even within the narrow confines
of this dance form, Haydn conjures something more than just politely bowing courtiers.

Fourth Movement: Over a single note, held
in octaves by the horns, the violas softly introduce the spirited and jolly tune *Red Hot
Buns,* popular in London in the 1790's. With
this catchy tune, Haydn has a merry time,
for he maneuvers it around in a manner
thoroughly delightful.

Michael Ippolitov-Ivanov

BORN 1859 NEAR ST. PETERSBURG, Russia, the
son of a mechanic employed in the manufac-
ture of candelabra and lamps for imperial
palaces. Studied under Rimsky-Korsakoff at
St. Petersburg Conservatory, following which
became director of music school at Tiflis in
the Caucasus. In 1906 became director of
Moscow Conservatory. Died 1935 (aged 75)
at Moscow; U. S. S. R.

CAUCASIAN SKETCHES
Suite for Orchestra Op. 10
FIRST PERFORMANCE: MOSCOW, FEBRUARY 5, 1895

In the course of his eleven years at Tiflis,
Ippolitov-Ivanov became deeply interested in
the native music of the different races
in the Caucasus. He undertook
research in the origin and
music and composed several w

Michael Ippolitov-Ivanov

growth of this study. Such a work is the suite *Caucasian Sketches*—a picturesque tone painting in which a distinctly Oriental coloring enters the composer's lyric, melodious style.

GUIDE TO LISTENING

1) *In The Mountains:* The opening bars sound a repeated horn call, transporting us into the wilderness of precipitous mountain ranges. Here is the Caucasus in all its rugged glory—deep canyons and snow capped peaks, galloping tribesmen, and long lines of mules creeping along narrow trails.

2) *In The Aoule:* (An "aoule"—accent on "ou"—is a Caucasian village). The plaintive song of the English horn, echoed by the viola, and the succeeding, drone-like, melancholy native dance, carry us into the heart of a Caucasian village. We see its white glistening walls, its mosque, its terraced roofs, its lithe, sun-tanned girls carrying water jugs.

3) *In The Mosque:* In this solemn music, the woodwinds and French horns usher us inside the portals of a mosque.

4) *Procession of the Sirdar:* (A "sirdar" is a native chieftain or official). The brilliantly martial music pictures the passage of the native chief and his retinue through a village in a vivid and clangorous procession.

Franz Liszt

Born 1811 at Raiding, Hungary, of noble descent, the son of a steward on the properties of the powerful Esterházy family. An infant prodigy, Liszt gave his first concert at nine and, after studying in Vienna, at twelve proceeded with his father to Paris where he was lionized. As he grew older, his amazing command of the piano—which has since become legendary—made him a world figure in music. Meantime, he grew famous also as a composer, and, during his succeeding career became an outstanding patron of creative artists, helping, among others, Richard Wagner, who married his daughter Cosima, born out of wedlock. In 1865 Liszt joined the Church in Rome where Pope Pius IX made him an abbé. This did not impede his career, for he pursued his worldly mode of life and numerous love affairs up to 1886 when he died (aged 74) of pneumonia at Beyreuth, Germany.

Regarding Liszt, the composer, it should be noted that he was the first to utilize the so-called "symphonic poem"—music which, though of symphonic proportions, is in one movement and is usually based on a literary conception. (For other works by Liszt see *Recommended Recordings*.)

LES PRELUDES
Symphonic Poem No. 3
FIRST PERFORMANCE: WEIMAR, FEBRUARY 23, 1854

Liszt was a fabulous personage, in more than one respect. For years his house was the center of musical Europe; to him composers and musicians of all kinds flocked by the hundred, like pilgrims to Mecca. With remarkable intuition he singled out the exceptionally gifted; with wonderful generosity he helped them and promoted their work wherever he could. It is through these activities, and, of course, through his playing, rather than through his compositions, that Liszt is particularly remembered—a truly towering figure in the Romantic era in which he lived.

Of Liszt's own music a good deal is superficially brilliant, verging on the bombastic. It is frankly display music; and Liszt, through

his career as a virtuoso pianist, certainly
knew what was effective and what was not.
It would be a mistake, though, to suppose
that surface brilliance was all Liszt was capable of, however much his popularity may
rest on his more superficial efforts. He was,
in fact, capable of rising to something greater
as is for instance evident in his impressive
Les Preludes, composed when he was in his
early forties. This symphonic poem was inspired by the *Méditations Poétiques,* a philosophical work of the nineteenth century
French poet Lamartine.

GUIDE TO LISTENING

The work opens with a melody of somber
majesty (later used by César Franck as the
opening and chief theme in his D minor
Symphony). This introduction ("What is
life but a series of preludes to that unknown
song whose initial notes are sounded in
death") takes on a bolder character before
it leads into a flowing passage ("The enchanted dawn of every life is love . . .")

But what is love if not an evanescent joy,
soon dispersed by the gathering storm? The
music seems to propound this question as
its mood darkens and it grows increasingly
agitated. When the storm is dispelled, we
hear a lovely rustic melody ("And what soul

thus severely bruised . . . does not seek to rest . . . in the calm of rural life?") Yet man allows himself no rest. At the trumpet call he hastens back into life's fray to test himself and to conquer. Surging resolutely, the music ends on this note of militant triumph.

Harp

Edward MacDowell

BORN 1861 AT NEW YORK CITY, a descendant of old Quaker family. Was early instructed in music and at fifteen traveled to study theory and piano in Paris (where he had Debussy as a fellow student) and to Germany where he also taught and composed. At twenty-six returned to America, already one of his country's outstanding composers. Was appointed in 1896 to fill Columbia University's first music professorship, but suffered in 1905 a complete mental collapse and died three years later (aged 46) in New York City. On his deathbed left request, later fulfilled by his widow, for the creation at Petersboro, N. H. of a permanent colony where creative artists could work in a congenial atmosphere and live at reduced cost.

MacDowell's music bears the stamp of poetic romanticism. It is pleasant music which combines refinement and virility with a certain freshness strongly suggestive of the open air—of wind-swept pastures and streams; of enchanted lakes reflecting legendary beings; of mysterious woods peopled by nymphs and dryads.

CONCERTO (PIANO AND ORCHESTRA) NO. 2
In D Minor, Op. 23
FIRST PERFORMANCE: NEW YORK CITY, MARCH 5, 1889

Edward MacDowell was a shy, sensitive man who found it hard to turn people away from his door or refuse their requests, both reasonable and unreasonable. When a stranger presented himself at his home in Wiesbaden, interrupting him in his work on the Second Piano Concerto, and insisted that he had to see the composer, MacDowell sighed but led the visitor into his study.

It appeared the man was an inventor. He had heard of MacDowell's presence in the city. He had also heard of the composition now in the process of being written, and he felt he could be of great assistance in the matter of completing the work. His research had enabled him to estimate just what combinations of tones had as yet been unused. In fact, he knew exactly how many more original melodies could be written, and these he would be glad to dispose of for a not too exorbitant price.

It has not been recorded whether Mac-Dowell bought himself a trunkful of melodies, but if he did, it is a fair guess that none of them found their way into his Second Piano Concerto.

GUIDE TO LISTENING

First Movement: After a quietly wistful introduction, the piano enters with a sudden cataract of sound from which emerges the first challenging theme. The music unfolds dramatically and with great verve. A quieter second theme, suggestive of endless moonlit vistas, brings the movement to a soft close.

Second Movement: This short movement overflows with a prodigious yet graceful exuberance. (MacDowell once sketched a symphonic poem inspired by a performance of *Much Ado About Nothing*. This remained unfinished, but much of the material intended for the Shakespearean tone poem later found its way into this movement.)

Third Movement: The introduction is pensive and built on themes of the first movement. But a defiant note is presently struck. It leads us by degrees to an exhilarating climax with which the work ends.

Felix Mendelssohn

BORN 1809 AT HAMBURG, Germany, the son of
a banker; grandson of a great Jewish scholar.
He absorbed music in the family circle and
gave his first piano concert at nine, becoming
noted for his improvisations at twelve. Beginning with the year of his graduation from
the Berlin University, when seventeen, embarked on a career as a composer and rose
quickly to a position of great popularity and
influence throughout Europe. After several
trips to England, where he was acclaimed,
became conductor of the Leipzig Gewandhaus
Orchestra. Retired in 1846 because of overwork, but his health nevertheless gave way
the following year when he died (aged 38)
at Leipzig.

Mendelssohn's music has refinement, clarity,
and radiance. Since it does not run deep,
this music is easy on the ear, but this is not
saying that it can be dismissed, as some
have tried to do, on the grounds that it is

superficial. For when it stays clear of sentimentality and is at its best, Mendelssohn's music has a sparkling charm and delicate precision which, in its special place, is intensely satisfying. (For other works by the composer see *Recommended Recordings*.)

EXCERPTS FROM "A MIDSUMMER NIGHT'S DREAM"
Incidental Music, Op. 21
FIRST PERFORMANCE: OVERTURE, STETTIN, FEBRUARY, 1827; ENTIRE WORK, POTSDAM, OCTOBER 14, 1843

Mendelssohn's youthful background must have been both fascinating and exhilarating. His younger sister sang; his brother played the 'cello; his older sister, Fanny, was almost as talented as he in composition, and perhaps even more accomplished as a pianist; and she was also very gifted as a water color artist. Their home was always filled with interesting people; and almost nightly, while the older folk foregathered to discuss literature and politics, the younger generation, including many friends who dropped in for the evening, formed themselves into a small orchestra, amidst much gayety. Felix and Fanny, two inseparables, took an active part in these activities. Together they also painted, played duets, philosophized, translated Shakespeare.

Mendelssohn was just seventeen when he wrote the remarkable overture to *A Midsummer Night's Dream*—improvising it, as he later confided "on the piano of a neighbor —a beautiful lady who lived near-by." The year was 1826. Later, in 1843, at the request of the King of Prussia, he wrote twelve additional numbers as incidental music to Shakespeare's play. Of these the Scherzo and the exquisite Nocturne are the best known.

GUIDE TO LISTENING

Overture: Is airy, youthful, permeated with a feeling of mischievous hobgoblins and dancing elfs. Occasionally broken into by strains of a broader, more heroic nature, the Overture ends in a rousing tune—a march that has escorted more young people to the altar than any comparable piece of music.

Nocturne: Is pensive in its limpid melody, lovely in its suggestion of the organ, even impassioned for a brief moment, though scarcely tragic at any point.

Scherzo: Is eerie, delicately spun, unfaltering in its gentle yet determined flow that ends as with a sigh.

Felix Mendelssohn

SYMPHONY NO. 4
In A Major, Op. 90 (Italian)
FIRST PERFORMANCE: LONDON, MAY 13, 1833

Mendelssohn was in the habit of translating into sound his impressions of the world, including the countries in which he traveled. His vivid recollections of England took the form of the Overture *Hebrides* and the *Scotch Symphony;* and those of stately Rome, beautiful Venice, and sunny Naples, were reflected in the *Italian Symphony.*

The latter was composed between 1831-33, and it was enthusiastically received. A hundred years have passed, but it is still a favorite, and it still sparkles with light-hearted vigor. Indeed, its effervescence persists in spite of time. This is the more remarkable when one considers the conditions of mental stress under which part of the work was written, for at the time when Mendelssohn was working on the Symphony, his nerves were taut, and he was smarting under the insult of his rejection as conductor by the membership of a Berlin choral society known as the *Sing Academie.* The rejection had been a blow, but what had really hurt was that in the action of the Society he had caught his first glimpse of the ugly specter of anti-Semitism.

GUIDE TO LISTENING

First Movement: The work opens with a rapidly moving theme that overflows with energy and life as it is given out by the violins, and carried along with increasing momentum by the entire orchestra. The brightness and verve of the music, and also its charm, are sustained to the end.

Second Movement: Is subdued and pensive, the principal melody voiced by clarinets, oboes, and violins, which enter after a brief introduction. This mood is maintained throughout the second theme as well as through the restatement of the first.

Third Movement: Is delicate, imaginative, and ingratiating in its elegance of style which is that of a minuet.

Fourth Movement: Is vivacious, bright, and youthful in its irresistible onward rush. It is written in the style of a *saltarelia*, which is an ancient Italian dance ("saltare" means to jump or skip). In this atmosphere of a lightly skipping dance the music courses along to a brilliant end.

Modeste Moussorgsky

BORN 1839 NEAR PSKOV, Russia, the son of a
landowner. Began his career as an officer of
the Guard, practicing music as an amateur.
At twenty-two met members of the then
budding Russian Nationalist School of composers, which he joined, resigning his commission. Later suffered general neglect and
poverty. Though largely self-taught, is perhaps the greatest composer Russia ever produced. Died 1881 (aged 42) at St. Petersburg, as biographer von Riesemann tells us,
"on a lonely death bed in a soldier's hospital"
where in order to be admitted he had to be
listed as an officer's servant.

The music of Moussorgsky speaks with a
force elemental and at times overwhelming.
Its accents are those of the people, and its
voice is unmistakably Russian. It has tenderness and glow, this voice, and it also has
anger, but its most salient characteristic is
its uncompromising directness—its expression

not of "beauty" so much as of "truth," as
Moussorgsky saw it. This is seen especially
in his songs—most of them musical minia-
tures of rare sensitivity and psychological in-
sight. (For other works by Moussorgsky see
Recommended Recordings.)

PICTURES AT AN EXHIBITION

COMPOSED ORIGINALLY FOR THE PIANO (1874).
LATER SCORED FOR ORCHESTRA, AMONG OTHERS
BY SIR HENRY WOOD, LUCIEN CAILLET, AND,
MOST SUCCESSFULLY, BY MAURICE RAVEL—THE LATTER
AT THE REQUEST OF SERGE KOUSSEVITZKY WHO
GAVE THE WORK ITS FIRST PERFORMANCE IN THIS
FORM AT PARIS, MAY 3, 1923

One summer day in the Eighteen-Seventies,
Moussorgsky was walking home with his close
friend Victor Hartman, a gifted architect,
then barely thirty-nine. At a street corner
the latter faltered and leaned against a wall.
Deliberately careless, the composer asked:

"What's up?"

"I can't breathe," gasped the stricken man.

Moussorgsky, who somehow already knew
that his friend's death warrant had been
signed, was seized with an overwhelming impulse to say something warm, something
friendly and comforting. But all he could

utter was a stiff: "We'll go on as soon as you feel a little better. . . ."

A short time later Hartman died, and his friends arranged an exhibit of his water colors and drawings to honor his memory. Moussorgsky, of course, attended. He felt keenly the loss of his friend, and he decided to compose a musical interpretation of some of the pictures. This he did in a single great spurt of creative invention. However, since he strove to achieve true characterizations of Hartman's pictures rather than mere salon pieces, pleasant to listen to but otherwise meaningless, he naturally violated prevalent convention.

This trespassing in the shrine of "musical beauty" was promtly seized upon by his contemporaries as another illustration of his musical uncouthness—of his lack of formal musical training. In fact, such pieces as the *Gnome*, or *Samuel Goldenberg and Schmuyle*, or even *Baba-Yaga's Hut*, were regarded as works of unparalleled and unforgivable audacity.

GUIDE TO LISTENING

Promenade: The broad, Russian melody with which the composition opens—Moussorgsky labeled it *The Promenade*—portrays the composer strolling through the exhibit.

Modeste Moussorgsky

The genial tune reappears from time to time, skillfully varied to fit the occasion.

1) *The Gnome:* (Hartman's picture shows a dwarf, hobbling clumsily.) There is something malevolent about the gnome—and the music—as he drags himself past us, glaring angrily out of the corner of his eye.

2) *The Old Castle:* (Picture shows a troubadour in front of a castle tower.) The song is long-drawn, melancholy, haunting.

3) *Tuileries:* (Picture shows alley in Tuileries gardens with nurses and children everywhere.) We hear the joyous confusion of chattering children and scolding nurses.

4) *Bydlo:* (Picture shows a primitive peasant wagon drawn by oxen.) Amidst the rumbling of the enormous wheels is heard the driver's swinging folk tune. The visitor watches the lumbering beasts as they pull the wagon away. He then resumes his *Promenade.*

5) *Ballet of Unhatched Chicken:* (Picture is a sketch of stage setting for the ballet Trilby.) A whimsical piece, and a great favorite with concert audiences.

6) *Samuel Goldenberg and Schmuyle:* (Picture shows two typical Warsaw Jews.) I want to "get" Hartman's Jews, wrote Moussorgsky to a friend; and he certainly got them—the one fat, prosperous, pompous;

the other lean, jittery, obsequious. The conversation between them—one of the voices whining, the other gruff and overbearing—is one of the masterstrokes of psychological writing in music.

7) *Market Place at Limoges:* (Picture shows a market place in South-Western France.) The visitor gazes briefly at this scene of confusion—of fish, vegetables, wrangling women, flowers and fruit—a typical market place—then he moves on to . . .

8) *Catacombs:* (Drawing by Hartman of himself examining interior of Paris catacombs.) As this solemn piece unfolds, we seem to see the mysterious reflections of a lantern on the wet subterranean walls.

9) *Baba-Yaga's Hut:* (Picture shows a hut perched on fowls' legs.) Moving in mighty forward spurts, the music suggests a witch's flight through the air on her gruesome errand—a search for human bones. (Baba-Yaga is a witch out of Russian folklore.)

10) *The Great Gate at Kieff:* (Picture shows architectural design of entrance gate for the city of Kieff). The musical setting is vaguely reminiscent of the *Promenade*, but more solid, as if to suggest the grandeur of the massive stone portals in this final picture at an exhibition.

Wolfgang Amadeus Mozart

BORN 1756 AT SALZBURG in the Bavarian Alps, the seventh child of a professional musician. Probably the greatest musical child genius we have had, he began to play the family clavichord at three; to compose at four; made his debut in Munich at six. This was the beginning of his early triumphs which took him all over Europe. At eighteen he had already three oratorios, nine masses, twenty-three sonatas, and many shorter works to his credit. At twenty-six he married Constanze Weber and settled in Vienna. Unfortunately both were fond of the nicer things in life, and though Mozart's income as a composer would compare favorably with that of any of our successful contemporaries, financial troubles multiplied. There followed several years of worry and overwork at the end of which his health gave way. Following a stroke in 1791 he died in Vienna (aged 35) and was buried in a pauper's grave.

Mozart's music is characterized by lucid ease and distinction of style which glistens with spontaneous brightness and grace. If we look beyond its polished surface, we often find a strength of fiber and a vibrancy of feeling which contradicts the popular concept of Mozart as a composer purely of "enchanted trivialities."

SYMPHONY NO. 40
In G Minor, K–550
FIRST PERFORMANCE: LEIPZIG, MAY, 1789

When he was married, Mozart, though twenty-six, was immature, aside from his music, and inexperienced in the ways of money. His bride was eight years younger, coquettish, frivolous, and a bit shallow. Both were inclined to live beyond their means, and their not too efficient way of keeping house did not decrease their difficulties. Mozart's job as court composer paid him poorly, but when they had money, received for numerous commissioned works, they spent it, understandably enough, on luxuries. When they had none, they barely managed, and their affairs were further complicated by the appearance, in quick succession, of six children, of whom four died in infancy.

During these years in Vienna, in spite of his creative productivity, Mozart sank ever deeper into debt. By 1788, when the famous G minor Symphony was written, he was reduced to sending frantic appeals to friends for an immediate loan. The young composer's plight was indeed desperate. His wife was ill; he was besieged by creditors; his home was in a dismal disarray. "God," he wrote in one of his appeals for money, "I am in a situation I would not wish on my worst enemy."

Some of the frantic overtones of this unhappy period of Mozart's short-lived career found their expression in the G minor Symphony. Yet if there is distress in this great Symphony, it never stoops to self-dramatization or self-pity, and of real tragedy there is no trace.

GUIDE TO LISTENING

First Movement: The work opens with a buoyant melody through whose fast-moving, surface elegance runs an undercurrent of tension. This mood deepens rather than lightens as the music unfolds, in turn wistful and sparkling alive, but always troubled as if with doubt or even sorrow.

Second Movement: Is permeated with serenity. It is lovely in its solemn tenderness and vibrant in its melancholy warmth as it moves unhurriedly to a subdued close.

Third Movement: Is resolute and vigorous. In form it is a minuet, but in content it exhibits a dramatic vigor completely alien to the superficial musical tastes of eighteenth century courtiers (who, in fact, looked askance at this, to them, strange kind of music).

Fourth Movement: Overflows with a high-strung, driving energy which finds no rest. A profoundly melancholy interlude serves only to emphasize the gloomy implications of the music which courses with scarcely a let-up to its sudden close.

SYMPHONY NO. 41
In C Major, K–551, (*Jupiter*)
FIRST PERFORMANCE: PROBABLY LEIPZIG, MAY, 1889

This is the last of Mozart's symphonies, and also the greatest, its scope and significance having earned for it the nickname *Jupiter.* The work is remarkable, too, purely as a feat of musical creation, for it was composed in about fourteen days. To accomplish this feat Mozart's flow of inspiration must have been prodigious, his sureness of touch beyond belief. Indeed he could not have done much re-writing, for the mere job

of getting the Symphony down on paper in
so short a time would have challenged the
dexterity of a professional copyist. But
Mozart, of course, was not merely copying
music. He was doing what, with special reference to this work, someone later characterized as "pure thinking in sound."

GUIDE TO LISTENING

First Movement: Opens at once on the principal theme which is resolute and stern, preparing us for the drama which is about to
unfold and to reach its climax in the last
movement. Before long a second, lighter
theme is introduced, but the feeling of suspense that was experienced from the start
is never quite dispelled.

Second Movement: Is slow, and it is also
exquisite in its melody which, deep-felt yet
restrained, is sung by the muted strings.
Presently the woodwinds join their voices to
those of the strings, and the lovely tonal
fabric broadens as the music reaches its close,
ending softly as if reluctant to break off.

Third Movement: Is a minuet. It is stately
yet gracefully playful, giving no intimation
of the emotional vehemence of the movement
that follows.

Fourth Movement: Opens with a melody that
is to form the basis of the entire movement.

This theme is broad and majestic, and on it Mozart builds a fugue of extraordinary scope and power. This fugue, which undoubtedly represents Mozart's greatest creative effort, culminates in a climax of towering finality.

Flute

Serge Prokofieff

BORN 1891 AT SONTSOVKA, his parents' estate in southern Russia. Already a composer at six, he outdistanced his music teachers, starting with his mother, as quickly as they could be supplied. At thirteen entered the St. Petersburg Conservatory where he studied under Rimsky-Korsakoff, graduating with high honors. Thereafter, in spite of bitter opposition to his modernism, rose steadily in prestige and finally attained world-wide recognition.

The modern and sophisticated personality of Prokofieff's music has many facets, and which of these will be displayed most prominently one never knows. One of them is the music's boldness, its driving force that verges on sheer ruthlessness. Another is its humor —which can be impish, teasing, or acrid in its bite. Still another is its recently acquired mellowness and lyricism, a tendency to speak more from the heart than from the intellect.

SYMPHONY

jor, Op. 25

FIRST P̶   ̶ETROGRAD, APRIL 21, 1918

It was during the early stages of the first
World War that Prokofieff first attracted no-
tice as the nightmare of musical academicians. With each new work from his precocious pen, conservative musicians shuddered
and critics rallied their most potent adjectives
to stem this terrible new music. But, if the
truth be told, the critics were not very candid.
What they really found abhorrent in Prokofieff was not his modernism, which they at-
tacked, but his directness, brutal and uncompromising—a truly diabolical knack of driving
straight at everything complacent, and blast-
ing it to bits.

That this was so, no one of course was
willing to admit. Instead, the critics raged
at what they called Prokofieff's "futurism."
One critic even went so far as to denounce a
new Prokofieff work without troubling to
hear it at a scheduled concert. This was
a sad mistake, for since the concert was can-
celled without warning, the critic found
himself exposed and lost his job.

At long last, weary of this ceaseless harry-

ing which sought to p███████is lack of
"soundness" was the r███████unsteady
grasp of the compo███████okofieff
doubly confounded his ███████writing
the *Classical Symphony*███████is Symphony, without yielding ███████of his characteristic manner of expression, he yet succeeded in adhering strictly to the classical
tradition, producing a work as polished in its
way as any that had ever come from a Mozart
or a Haydn.

GUIDE TO LISTENING

First Movement: The work starts with a melody in the violins which shuffles brightly
along, its whole course punctuated by energetic chords. When it is done, a contrasting
theme is introduced—sparse, biting, elegantly
turned—and now the music unfolds briskly
to the very end.

Second Movement: Opens slowly, tentatively,
with a melody that starts on one of the high
notes of the violin. Twice this melody reappears, varied to suit the occasion.

Third Movement: Is an extremely graceful
gavotte which is as wily in its feeling of
modernity as it is perfect in its classical form.

Fourth Movement: Is virile, straightforward,
gaining steadily in momentum and exuberance as it courses to its brilliant end.

Sergei Rachmaninoff

BORN 1873, ON AN ESTATE NEAR NOVGOROD, Russia. At nine, when his parents separated, was taken by his mother to St. Petersburg and there enrolled at the College of Music. Later became a student at the Moscow Conservatory, a protégé and spiritual disciple of Tchaikowsky. At nineteen composed his C-sharp minor Prelude which, though a minor effort, spread his fame to the four corners of the world. For a time undecided as to whether to take up piano playing or composition as his major activity, finally settled on the former, especially after he left Russia in 1918. Yet through the years, though producing little, Rachmaninoff has been growing steadily in stature as a composer.

Rachmaninoff's music is probably the most nostalgic music of the day—a by-gone day, to be exact, of a by-gone Russia. Still, for all its unrelieved, soul-scathing pessimism, its listless melodies, its tendency to keep repeating the same thing, this music bears up well under repeated hearings. It has the ring of absolute sincerity, and its sincerity is eloquent because it leaves so much unsaid. (For other works by Rachmaninoff see *Recommended Recordings*.)

CONCERTO (PIANO AND ORCHESTRA) NO. 2

In C Minor, Op. 18

FIRST PERFORMANCE: MOSCOW, OCTOBER 14, 1901

"America" played an important part in Rachmaninoff's life even before the fateful events which brought the composer to the New World. "America" was the name of the lodging establishment where Rachmaninoff stayed while enjoying the unexpected success of his famous prelude; while agonizing, too, over his fitness as a composer, following the abject failure of his First Symphony.

Of this unhappy work for which Rachmaninoff had entertained the fondest hopes, one critic tersely said: "If there were a Conservatory of Music in Hell, Rachmaninoff would receive from it the first prize for his Symphony." This fiasco rankled the composer. It rankled not so much because the work had proved a failure, as because after "agonizing hours of doubt" it had brought Rachmaninoff to the conclusion that he was "unfitted" for composing, and that it would be best "to put an end to it at once."

For almost two years Rachmaninoff did next to nothing. He saw practically no one. He wrote practically no music. He spent his time mostly alone, with his pet dog as sole companion, reclining on the couch a prey to an unconquerable torpor.

At last, unable to rid himself of his strange apathy, he had recourse to a physician, Dr. Dahl, a forerunner of Coué, whose method of suggestion and auto-suggestion had been called miraculous by former patients. After three months of daily treatments, Rachmaninoff was cured. On the rebound, he wrote a work which "out of gratitude" he dedicated to Dr. Dahl. It was his Second Piano Concerto—a composition which has since risen to the very top, usurping in public favor the very place previously occupied by the famous *B-flat minor Concerto* of Rachmaninoff's famous teacher, Tchaikowsky.

GUIDE TO LISTENING

First Movement: The piano, which starts off alone, gently at first but with increasing vigor, is joined dramatically by the orchestra in a statement of the sweeping and lofty first theme. After a short but tense development, the second theme is reached—a dreamy and poetic melody which, by contrast with the first theme, seems almost intimate. Soon the original mood returns, and the music then rises with funereal splendor to several impassioned climaxes.

Second Movement: Is subdued in coloring, restrained in its hazily motionless, half-slumbering melody, extremely moving in its quietly dignified way. Briefly the music is agitated, as if a stormy gust of wind had swept through it, but it soon relapses into its original mood of quietly impassioned singing.

Third Movement: The opening is brilliant and spirited. It leads to an eloquently lyrical passage, but the music quickly reverts to its opening bravura style and proceeds in this fashion as though fighting a duel with itself —a duel between a youthful vigorousness of outlook and an intensely solemn kind of pessimism.

SYMPHONY NO. 2
In E Minor, Op. 27
FIRST PERFORMANCE: MOSCOW, WINTER 1908–09

When he was in his early twenties, Rachmaninoff found few opportunities to add to his income by playing the piano. He was regarded as a promising young composer, and the accepted view was that composers seldom made good pianists. When he sat down to play, usually to introduce some compositions of his own, people remarked on his fine playing. They seemed surprised that he could play at all.

A few years later, when the exceptional qualities of Rachmaninoff's playing had gained wider recognition, people reversed themselves. For now they argued that a pianist seldom had the makings of a real composer. Rachmaninoff's music, they said, was most unusual—for a pianist—but its affinity to the great Tchaikowsky made it quite clear that the young man was primarily a pianist, not a composer. In the words of that astute critic Sabaneyev: *

"This extraordinary pianist with a rhythm of steel, with mighty and tender tone, with hands superhuman, like those of Liszt, and with a temperament that could engulf the temperaments of all the pianists of the present day . . . cast a heavy shadow over his own image as a composer. . . ."

But Rachmaninoff *was* a composer. He persevered. "Indisputably," says Sabaneyev,

---

* Leonid Sabaneyev in "Modern Russian Composers"—International Publishers, N. Y.

Sergei Rachmaninoff

"Rachmaninoff matured. . . . Tchaikowsky's image vanishes little by little, obscured by the image of Rachmaninoff himself. This latter image is not all-embracing, is not broad. . . . Rachmaninoff is far 'narrower' than Tchaikowsky. But psychologically he is greater. . . . This 'greatness of a man' is neither the merit of his creative work, nor the size of his compositions. One can be the author of huge symphonies and be little, and again compose preludes and be vast. One may compose poor music, yet be 'great' in spirit, and in this poor music this greatness will still come forward in some mysterious way. . . . Rachmaninoff is a man of great spirit. . . . By the same mysterious standard Rachmaninoff surpasses his genius-endowed teacher, Tchaikowsky. . . . He lives through his limited experience with infinite, with titanic force . . ." alongside of which "Tchaikowsky's lyricism appears 'commoner'" for, as Sabaneyev further points out: "In Rachmaninoff's darkness there is still more impenetrableness as well as more majesty and solemnity."

These words were written in 1927. Ten years later, when asked to give their opinion on what living composers they thought would be played a hundred years hence, the American radio audience voted Rachmaninoff in third place, with only Sibelius and Strauss ahead of him.

GUIDE TO LISTENING

First Movement: After a short, ominous introduction intoned by the 'cellos and double-basses, we hear the first theme of the movement. It is grieving and heroic, like some passionate cry wrung from the very depths of the soul. In this mood the music develops, gradually subsiding in its anguish—its second theme at first more objective and restrained—but rising again to a great climax of gloomy intensity.

Second Movement: This movement is bustling, agitated. It is furiously vigorous without being gay; exciting and yet, underneath, somehow inexorable—its second, contrasting theme flowing along like some mighty river, its arms unfurled over thousands of miles, its past buried in the mists of prehistoric Russia.

Third Movement: This is the slow movement of the Symphony, and we are at once introduced to its chief theme—a melody of haunting splendor and great loveliness. All of Rachmaninoff's love for and identification with Russia is revealed in this music which achieves heights of nostalgic ecstasy he has not since duplicated.

Sergei Rachmaninoff

Fourth Movement: This movement acts as a summation but with a resurgence of spirit, for its opening theme is martial and its accents are those of triumph. We hear echoes from the preceding movements, but these are soon dissipated, and the music resumes its march-like forward sweep, culminating in a brilliantly effective end.

Double Bass

Maurice Ravel

BORN 1875 AT CIBOURE in France, not far
from the Spanish frontier. Although as a
child showed no startling musical gifts, was
encouraged at twelve to study the piano by
his father, an engineer and musical amateur.
In time entered the Paris Conservatory. He
was twenty-three when his work received its
first public performance, but recognition was
delayed because of sharp hostility from the
musical pundits of the time. Nevertheless,
in spite of many official slights, Ravel rose
steadily, achieving with the years eminence
as a composer, eventually even international
fame. In 1933 was stricken with a brain
ailment and died three years later (aged 62)
in a Paris clinic.

Ravel's music is modern in idiom and fastidious in content. It is invariably well-
tailored and well-groomed, and it has a
delicate finesse, a luminosity, and a sophisticated precision which have tempted compari-

son with a formal French garden in which the trees and shrubs and flowers are all neatly trimmed and perfectly laid out in symmetrical balance. Although this music, with its overtones of irony, does not probe deeply, it is the handiwork of a superlative craftsman. (For some of the composer's other works, see *Recommended Recordings*.)

DAPHNIS AND CHLOÉ
Second Orchestral Suite, Drawn from the Ballet, Similarly Named
FIRST PERFORMANCE: PARIS, JUNE 8, 1912

With the bright light of Debussy's star in their eyes, people for years payed relatively little heed to Ravel. Because the two men were contemporaries; because both had embarked along unexplored paths; and because their compositions displayed superficial resemblances, the music of both Frenchmen was for a long time considered by the public as almost indistinguishable. But since Debussy came first (he was Ravel's senior by thirteen years; had his first challenging work —his string quartet—performed when Ravel was still a junior student at the Paris Conservatory), it was he who was deemed the originator—Ravel, the imitator.

This erroneous impression, though still widely entertained, is being gradually corrected. The change has been speeded by the appearance in 1928 of that musical bestseller, the *Bolero*. For the phenomenal popular success of this piece, by increasing the demand for performances of Ravel's other works, has helped people perceive the essential difference in the musical personalities of the two men—Debussy, a composer inclining toward a sensuous dreaminess, an elusive quality all his own, and Ravel leaning in the opposite direction of sharp-edged definiteness, acrid humor, and sophisticated restraint even when treating the picturesque as in the *Daphnis and Chloé* music.

Ravel composed this music as a ballet for Diaghileff's famous company of dancers in Paris. In this form the work was not too well received. Its two concert versions were more successful, especially the *Second Suite*, now rated as very popular, indeed.

The music of this suite depicts incidents of an ancient Greek tale whose principal characters are the young lovers Daphnis and Chloé.

GUIDE TO LISTENING

Daybreak—Pantomime—General Dance: Only the murmur of water that drips from the rocks is heard as Daphnis, in a stupor, lies stretched out before the grotto of the Nymphs. Dawn is breaking. Birds are heard. Shepherds call to one another. They rouse Daphnis just as his beloved Chloé enters surrounded by shepherdesses. She has just escaped the pirates, who had abducted her, through the intervention of the god, Pan; and now, together with Daphnis, she mimes the story of the god Pan and the nymph Syrinx, whom Pan loved. In the role of Pan, Daphnis makes love to Chloé, is repulsed, then fashions a flute on which he plays. Chloé, impersonating the Nymph, whirls to the tune, finally falls into Daphnis' arms. Rejoicing follows and a general dance by all those present.

BOLERO
A Solo Ballet
FIRST PERFORMANCE: PARIS, NOVEMBER 1928

Ravel was once regarded as a "dreadful modernist"—a willful "perpetrator of ugly music." How ironic that he should have been the one to produce the *Bolero*, "that tonal oil-gusher which is making him a plutocrat," as Lawrence Gilman at the time remarked.

It is to be doubted if any musical composition ever before attained a comparable degree of popularity in so many quarters at once—among highbrow and lowbrow; in vaudeville and concert hall; in theater and on the air; at Rome, Cairo, Paris, and New York. Needless to say, Ravel, who had composed all his life for a limited audience, was thunderstruck by this sudden acclaim (which his better works never enjoyed)—especially by the scope of this acclaim. He had written the *Bolero* to order for the Parisian dancer Ida Rubinstein and her company. He thought that this would be the end of it.

The scene of the Ballet is an inn in Spain. On a table surrounded by spectators, a woman executes a Spanish dance accompanying herself with castanets. The spectators, at first calm, work themselves up into a frenzy as the dance nears its climax.

GUIDE TO LISTENING

A languid Spanish dance theme, consisting of two closely related melodies, is repeated over and over in a manner remarkable for its variety of instrumental coloring.

First the snare drum softly hammers out the rhythm of the dance. Above this inexorable rhythm the melody appears, sounded in turn by different instruments—first singly, then in groups—gradually mounting in volume and electrifying effect until a climax is reached that is irresistibly rousing when heard for the first time.

Kettledrums

Nicholas Rimsky-Korsakoff

BORN 1844 AT TIHVIN, Russia, of noble birth with peasant blood from both grandmothers, one of them a serf. Early showed musical leanings, although dreaming of a career as a sailor. At eighteen graduated from Naval Academy and sailed on extended training cruise. Returning, renewed formerly brief acquaintance with Balakireff, young leader of movement to "russianize Russian music," and began to compose in earnest. On the strength of these early efforts, though totally ignorant in matters of musical theory, was appointed, at twenty-seven, professor of composition at St. Petersburg Conservatory. After bluffing his way along, undertook serious study, becoming in time a scholarly composer, outstanding as "the father of twentieth century orchestration." Died 1908 (aged 64) at St. Petersburg, Russia.

Rimsky-Korsakoff's music is largely de-

scriptive; its subject matter, mostly Slavonic
folk legend; its strong points, fastidious
craftsmanship and a masterly use of orchestral color. At its best it is picturesque, animated, brilliantly suggestive of the East,
especially legendary Russia.

SCHEHERAZADE

Symphonic Suite (After *The Thousand
And One Nights*) , Op. 35

FIRST PERFORMANCE: ST. PETERSBURG, WINTER
1888–89

To speak of Rimsky-Korsakoff as an industrious man is to be guilty of an under-
statement. For to achieve erudition in music,
such as he did, after a late start; to compose
three symphonies, fifteen operas, and a score
of other, lesser works, while at the same time
conducting, teaching, and acting as Inspector
of Naval Bands; to find time, in between, to
write two textbooks and an autobiography—
the latter, without the benefit of noticeable
literary gifts ("Stumbling, halting, perspir-
ing," says Carl Van Vechten, "Rimsky-Korsakoff put down the truth as he saw it . . .") ;
to add to all this the mean task—but to him
a labor of love—of scoring or re-editing sev-

eral orphan works left unfinished by three
other major Russian composers—to such a
giant of tireless industry only the word prodigious can do justice.

Clearly, such a man must have turned
everything in his life to proper account. Indeed, we owe some of his best descriptive passages to this capacity—the sea in *Scheherazade,*
for instance—surely a musical expression of
his vivid impression as a naval officer in the
tropics. ("The ocean glistened," he wrote in
his autobiography. "Flying fish leaped about
. . . The color of the sky, deep-blue by day,
was replaced at night by an indescribably
luminous glow. . . .").

The story of *Scheherazade,* drawn from the
Arabian Nights, is concerned with the powerful Sultan Schariar who, convinced of all
women's unfaithfulness, decides to put his
wives to death. One of these, Scheherazade,
saves herself by spinning colorful yarns which,
stretching over one thousand and one nights
in the telling, so intrigue the Sultan that he
changes his mind and spares her life.

GUIDE TO LISTENING

The sternly menacing theme of the opening bars portrays the all-powerful Sultan. It
is succeeded by the voluptious voice of

Scheherazade, a theme played by a solo violin.
She is about to weave her first tale of adventure; and now—a wonderfully undulating
rhythm, like the swell of some distant, coral-
studded sea, surges up from the orchestra,
conjuring visions of a lonely ship sailing on
its tropical voyage. Briefly, we later again
hear the Sultan's stern voice, but Scheherazade goes on with the next tale—a tale of the
mendicant monk Kalender, portrayed when
first introduced by a wistfully oriental melody
in the solo bassoon. Several more colorful
stories are unfolded before us, and finally, we
again hear the sea where the ship has been
wrecked on the craggy shores over which
watches the legendary figure of the Bronze
Warrior.

THE GOLDEN COCKEREL
Symphonic Suite Drawn from the Opera-
Pantomime, Similarly Named
OPERA'S FIRST PERFORMANCE, MOSCOW, SEPTEM-
BER 24, 1909

Rimsky-Korsakoff never heard his last
work, *The Golden Cockerel* (*Coq d'Or*) which
he composed in 1907. The Tzar's government, construing the opera as a satire on Im-

perial Russia and its institutions, forbade its performance and did not relax the ban until after the composer's death. (Although performed elsewhere in Russia, the ban was actually never lifted at the Imperial Opera House in St. Petersburg).

The story of the Golden Cockerel, based on a poem by Pushkin, concerns itself with the ridiculous goings-on at the imaginary court of the decadent King Dodon. From an aged astrologer, the king secures a magic bird—a Golden Cockerel with the power to warn of danger to the kingdom. Thereupon the King takes a nap, but no sooner has he gone to sleep than the Cockerel starts crowing. Reluctantly, the king gets up and sends his two sons to battle the invader. Shortly the Cockerel is again heard crowing, and the King, though grieved, sets forth himself.

He discovers that the "invader" is a beautiful Queen, and that because of her charms his two sons have killed each other. The pompous King himself succumbs to the Queen and conducts her back to the capital. At this juncture, the astrologer steps forward and claims his reward. He wants the Queen. Furious, King Dodon strikes him down. The magic Cockerel then swoops down on him and kills him with his sharp beak.

Nicholas Rimsky-Korsakoff

Introduction and Prologue—Slumber Scene and Warning: The Suite opens with the piercing theme of the Cockerel, sounded by a muted trumpet. We hear snatches of the famous *Hymn to the Sun* and the piping theme of the Astrologer. The music then switches to the *Slumber Scene.*

Prelude to Act 2—King Dodon's Arrival: Lugubrious chords, punctuated by shrill outbursts by the piccolo, and coupled with the somber strains of a march, depict the King's arrival at the scene of battle and his aggrieved lamentations.

Dance of the King and Queen: The violas intone the languorous music to which the Queen dances. Fascinated, the King watches. As he attempts to join in the dance, the music quickens and changes in character from the seductive to the ridiculous.

Bridal March and Death of King: The opening gloomy bars depict the populace awaiting the King's return. Again the Cockerel sounds his warning; and now the King and Queen make their appearance to the strains of a tremendous march which conjures the whole pompous, colorful procession. The music culminates in Dodon's death.

Gioacchino Rossini

Born 1792 at pesaro, Italy, the son of a town trumpeter who also was a slaughter house inspector. Early was apprenticed to a blacksmith, but, greatly gifted for music, picked up its rudiments where and as he could, working in churches as singer and in theaters as cembalo player. At fifteen composed a cantata; at seventeen a successful comic opera. Thereafter, in rapid succession, wrote thirty-eight operas from which he reaped great popularity. In 1824 moved to Paris where he became director of the *Théatre Italien*. By this time he was world famous, but, at thirty-seven, while at the height of his career, he retired from the field, presumably to enjoy life and avoid the strain to which he had been subjected in composing his last opera, *William Tell*. An epicure and a gourmet, Rossini spent the remainder of his life composing little but living well, his house a meeting place for the intellectual and artistic élite of Paris. Died 1868 (aged 79) at Paris.

Rossini's music combines an elegant and sparkling melodiousness with clarity, and both of these with laughter. Its wit, however, is not always playful, for it is often slyly devastating, even steely, in its thrust. (For other works by the composer see *Recommended Recordings*.)

OVERTURE TO "THE BARBER OF SEVILLE"

FIRST PUBLIC PERFORMANCE: ROME, FEBRUARY, 1816

According to legend Rossini composed his opera *The Barber of Seville* in thirteen days. When asked if such a feat were possible, the composer Donizetti is said to have replied: "Why not—Rossini is so lazy."

There was some truth in this remark. Although hard-working when really pressed, Rossini would have traded action for inaction any time. When the manuscript of the Overture to the *Barber of Seville* was lost, he did not trouble to reconstruct it. Instead, he pulled out of his trunk a piece he had already used to introduce two previous operas dealing with such dissimilar subjects as the adventures of the Roman Emperor Aurelian and the predicaments of Queen Elizabeth of England. This handy "substitute" became the piece which the whole world now knows as *Barber of Seville Overture*.

GUIDE TO LISTENING

A resounding chord introduces this effervescent overture. Toward the end the music gradually increases in volume in an exciting crescendo, following which the Overture ends with a flourish.

Clarinet

Camille Saint-Saëns

BORN 1835 AT PARIS, France. Showed early a fondness for music and a remarkable gift for the piano. At seven, already a composer, was admitted to the Paris Conservatory from which he graduated with honors. Thereafter embarked on a long career as organist, pianist, conductor, writer, and, above all, as a versatile and prolific composer, in time becoming one of the most eminent musicians of France. Died 1921 (aged 86) in Algiers.

The music of Saint-Saëns is lucid, brilliant, and essentially Gallic. Though not hard to woo, for it does not run very deep, it makes up by its polish and sparkle what it lacks in profundity.

CONCERTO (PIANO AND ORCHESTRA) NO. 4
In C Minor, Op. 44

FIRST PERFORMANCE: PARIS, OCTOBER 31, 1875

When Saint-Saëns emerged from the Paris Conservatory and became, at twenty-three, the organist at the church of St. Madelaine, he had fire in his eye and a musical chip on his shoulder. Forthwith he took a young woman to task because she, a prospective bride, begged him not to play austere fugues at her wedding. And when one of the parish priests undertook to explain to him that light music had much to recommend it since the congregation, being wealthy, derived its musical tastes from the Opéra Comique, young Saint-Saëns, according to Richard Aldrich, is alleged to have retorted:

"Monsieur l'Abbé, when I hear from the pulpit the language of the Opéra Comique, I will play music appropriate to it, and not before."

With ripening years this youthful mood, like a rich vintage properly aged, turned to genial mellowness, but we still catch echoes of it in the final movement of this piano concerto which Saint-Saëns wrote in his fortieth year.

GUIDE TO LISTENING

First Movement: The introduction—an extended dialogue between piano and orchestra—leads directly to a passage of earnest, almost religious character. This contemplative mood reaches, toward the end of the movement, a quiet fervor that is extremely expressive.

Camille Saint-Saëns

Second Movement: This is lively music, yet light and containing overtones of maliciousness. Later a melody with the freshness of a folk song provides a contrasting interlude. It leads to a dashing conclusion with some dazzling pianistic display.

CARNIVAL OF ANIMALS
A Grand Zoological Fantasy for Orchestra
FIRST HEARD IN PRIVATE PERFORMANCE: PARIS, FEBRUARY, 1887

In his mature years Saint-Saëns became known as a wit, but a cautious wit, seldom if ever indulging his sense of humor at the possible expense of professional considerations. Thus, though the fifty-two-year-old composer undoubtedly delighted in the creation of his satirical *Carnival of Animals,* he forbade its public performance soon after its introduction at a privately held concert as a surprise for the carnival season.

Even so, serious musicians raised their eyebrows. But they had no cause for worry. The Suite was not heard from again until 1922 when, after the composer's death, a clause was found in his will, lifting the ban. Only one of the numbers, *The Swan,* escaped this prohibition and became a favorite salon piece, played on every occasion by every small orchestra throughout the world.

Camille Saint-Saëns

1) *Introduction and Royal March of the Lion:* An ominous introduction ushers the martial procession in which the roaring King of Beasts is paraded past a gaping public.

2) *Hens and Cocks:* Cackling hens, crowing cocks, and other familar sounds of the barnyard are here cleverly imitated.

3) *Hemiones* (wild asses): A rapid, expressionless piano passage conjures visions of the galloping beasts—or intimates, perhaps, that piano players who play in this fashion are themselves galloping asses.

4) *Tortoises:* This is a parody on a well known tune from Offenbach's *Orpheus in Hades.* Usually played in break-neck fashion, it is here presented at truly tortoise speed.

5) *The Elephant:* The heavy, lumbering tread of the elephant projected through a humorous tune in the double-basses, is mingled with ironic echoes of the Waltz of the Sylphs from Berlioz' *Damnation of Faust.*

6) *Kangaroos:* A delicately jumpy tune by the two pianos provides a quaint tone picture of this animal in a cage at the zoo.

7) *Aquarium:* This piece suggests the movement of glimmering fish in the translucent water of the aquarium.

8) *Personages With Long Ears:* Who these personages are is clearly indicated by the music.

9) *Cuckoo in the Woods:* The clarinet and piano unite in this forest scene that has a familiar ring.

10) *Birds:* The flute and piano flit and chirp in a realistic tone picture of the zoo's aviary.

11) *Fossils:* Several well known tunes, among them Saint-Saëns' own *Danse Macabre,* are woven into this clever parody.

12) *The Swan:* This perennially favorite salon piece is gracefully voiced by the 'cello.

13) *The Pianists:* This is an ironic comment on the playing of finger exercises, suggesting perhaps that those who overdo the exercises really belong in the zoo.

14) *Finale:* A recapitulation of all that came before is proclaimed in true carnival spirit ending in a climax of scintillating vigor.

Violin

Ernest Schelling

BORN 1876 AT BELVEDERE, New Jersey, of Swiss parentage. Was a child prodigy and entered Paris Conservatory before he was eight. Later studied at the University of Pennsylvania and under Paderewski in Switzerland. At twenty-seven toured Europe and South America as pianist composer, and, from 1917–20 served with the U. S. Army in France. After the war became especially widely known as the conductor of the N. Y. Philharmonic Orchestra's Children's Concerts. Died 1939 (aged 63) in New York.

A VICTORY BALL
Fantasy for Orchestra
FIRST PERFORMANCE: PHILADELPHIA, FEBRUARY 23, 1923

When Major Schelling left active service in 1920, the horrors of war still haunted his imagination. Upon his return to America, he was amazed to find "that so few seemed to remember what the war really had meant, with its sacrifice of life and youth." When a poem by Alfred Noyes describing the war dead watching a victory ball given by the living came to his attention, Schelling was impelled to set it to music.

GUIDE TO LISTENING

The mood of mystery which hangs over the opening bars is pierced by discordant echoes of a martial character, as if to suggest a deserted battlefield on the night following the battle. But soon the spirit of the music changes, transporting us to a brilliantly lighted ballroom. We hear a polonaise, a suggested tango, as the frivolous, swirling crowd makes merry.

At the height of the revelry there is a sudden hush. A trumpet call, a roll of the drums—then, from the haunting distance outside, coming nearer and nearer, the measured tread of the dead. On they come, these ghostly legions, to partake in the feast. Closer and closer they draw, their oncoming heralded by trumpet calls.

The revelers throw themselves into the intoxicating swing of a waltz and momentarily succeed in drowning the horrible vision.

They drink and they dance, trying to ignore the presence of their dead comrades. But the ghostly apparition reasserts itself. There is a dramatic drum-roll which slowly dies away. Then, from far off, a trumpeter's mournful voice is heard playing "Taps."

Trumpet

Franz Schubert

BORN 1797 IN VIENNA, the twelfth child of a poor schoolmaster. At eight learned the rudiments of music from his father. Possessed of a beautiful voice, won at eleven a fellowship at a Jesuit school where he stayed for several years, singing in the Imperial choir and, at sixteen, composing his first symphony. On leaving the school became a schoolmaster, partly to avoid military conscription, partly because his father desired it. Meanwhile continued to compose. Extremely prolific, he wrote, among other things, a symphony, two masses, several string quartets, and nearly one hundred fifty songs when still in his eighteenth year. Earned his first money from his music the following year and stopped teaching but remained miserably poor throughout his life, living most of the time on the bounty of one or another of his friends. In 1828 arranged the first and only concert devoted to his works. Died the same year (aged 31) of typhus in Vienna.

Schubert was primarily a song writer—one of the greatest if not the greatest—and his extraordinary lyrical gift overshadows everything else in his music. In his symphonies melodies tender and poignant, flow with seemingly inexhaustible inspiration.

SYMPHONY NO. 8
In B Minor (*Unfinished*)
FIRST PERFORMANCE: VIENNA, DECEMBER 17, 1865

Although this symphony bears the nickname "unfinished" and consists of only two instead of the conventional four movements, it is decidedly "finished" in terms of what it has to say. This, notwithstanding the efforts of a misguided organization which, to celebrate the Schubert centennial in this country in 1928, offered ten thousand dollars to the composer who would complete the Symphony.

The story of the work is curious. In 1823 Schubert was elected to the membership of a musical society in Graz. Touched by this gesture, the composer wrote back, saying he would send the score of a new symphony in token of his gratitude. A year later, reminded of this promise by his father, Schubert sent the society the score of what is now

known as the *Unfinished Symphony*. This
score came into the possession of the director
of the society, one Aselm Huttenbrenner, who
kept it for forty-two years before he men-
tioned it to any one, although he made a
piano arrangement of the score for his own
use. Needless to say, Schubert never heard
the Symphony, a work destined to rise to
great heights of popular favor when it was
discovered and performed, years after its
composer's tragic death.

GUIDE TO LISTENING

First Movement: The opening bars of the
Unfinished Symphony, though somber, are
soon succeeded by an agitated passage which
leads out into the statement of one of the
best known and best loved melodies in all
symphonic music. From this point the music
progresses through several climaxes of vary-
ing intensity and winds up in a succession of
four great chords.

Second Movement: Starts off with a flowing
melody of great loveliness, given out by
French horns, bassoons, and strings. We
hear next a second theme which is both tender and resigned. The music then becomes
more dramatic, but not for very long, for
the original mood reasserts itself, and in this
atmosphere of peace the Symphony ends.

Robert Schumann

BORN 1810 AT ZWICKAU, Germany, the son of an author-bookseller. Started composing at six and soon began setting his own poems to music. After completing studies in law and philosophy at the University of Leipzig, decided to become an outstanding piano virtuoso, but in his overzeal in training his fingers, crippled one of them. This turned him to composition and to musical criticism, which proved no less remarkable than his music. After marrying Clara Wieck, daughter of his piano teacher and an outstanding musician in her own right, gained a European reputation with his *Quintet Op. 44.* Subject to exhaustion and fits of depression, threw himself into the Rhine at forty-four and had to be placed in an insane asylum at Eudenich, where he died (aged 46) in 1856, one of the most eminent of German composers.

Schumann's music is imaginative, whimsical, youthfully exuberant, filled with a naturalness and ease and a freshness seemingly inexhaustible. Endowed with a remarkable sense of and for the piano, Schumann is at his best in compositions in which that instrument plays an important part.

SYMPHONY NO. 1
In B-Flat Major, Op. 38 (*Spring*)
FIRST PERFORMANCE: LEIPZIG, MARCH 31, 1841

Robert Schumann was, if not the actual leader, then at least the most brilliant spokesman of the romantic movement in music which developed in the first half of the Nineteenth Century.

What the romanticists were after, and what they preached and practiced, was a shift in emphasis in what was to be considered paramount in composing music—content or form? To the technically minded musicians of the time, perfection in music's structural design was the important thing. To the romanticists this was a secondary issue. To them the primary consideration was emotional appeal. In their music they therefore leaned more toward the personal, subjective, and descriptive, as with Liszt, Berlioz, Chopin, Mendelssohn, and Schumann.

Outside of the labors connected with his

Robert Schumann

tremendous musical output, Schumann found time between 1834 and 1844 to edit the *Neue Zeitschrift,* a musical bi-weekly, in which he lashed against mere technical proficiency and superficial brilliance in music; acted as herald to young geniuses, such as Brahms; and ardently crusaded for the "romantic" cause. He wrote the *Spring Symphony* in a single month, on an upsurge of inspiration following shortly upon his marriage, "in that flush of spring," as he said, "which carries a man away even in his old age. . . ."

GUIDE TO LISTENING

First Movement: The work opens with a limpid call by trumpets and French horns which, so Schumann wrote, he intended "to sound as if from on high, like a summons to awakening." In what follows, he also said, he meant to "assemble everything that belongs to Spring—the sprouting green of trees, even the fluttering of butterflies."

Second Movement: Is slow and tenderly impassioned.

Third Movement: Is energetic, full-blooded, teeming with the vitality of youth.

Fourth Movement: Is light-hearted, fast-moving, dance-like. "I should like to think of it as Spring's Farewell . . . not to be rendered frivolously," wrote Schumann.

◇◇◇◇◇◇◇◇◇◇◇◇◇◇◇◇◇◇◇◇◇◇◇◇◇◇◇◇◇◇

Jean Sibelius

BORN 1865 AT TAVASTEHUS, Finland, of Finnish-
Swedish stock, the son of an army surgeon.
As a boy excelled in his studies, especially in
mathematics and, above all, in music, for he
wanted to be a violin virtuoso. Decided to
become a composer when in his second year
as a law student at the University of
Helsingfors, and thereupon entered that city's
Music Conservatory before going to Berlin, at
twenty-four, to continue his studies in composition. Returning to Finland, was married
and, at twenty-six, scored his first great local
success as a composer. Five years later was
granted by the Finnish Government an annual
pension which was later increased and guar-
anteed for the duration of his life. Thereafter, with the exception of occasional trips
abroad, lived quietly in Finland, composing
and slowly making his mark as the most
monumental figure in twentieth century
symphonic music.

The music of Sibelius has all the properties that distinguish great music, and its occasional lapses into triviality or sentimentality are beside the point: one does not quibble with the voice that speaks with such intensity and sweep. The world from which Sibelius speaks seems of a tougher fiber than our world today. This is felt sometimes with overwhelming force in the background of the music, often austere and elemental, prone to suggest immensities imponderable, and given to incalculable silences.

SYMPHONY NO. 1
In E Minor, Op. 39
FIRST PERFORMANCE: HELSINGFORS, APRIL 26, 1899

On the memorable day when this Symphony was played for the first time, Sibelius joined in spirit the company of such illustrious patriots as Smetana and Verdi. On that day the people of Finland first realized that they had among them not merely a composer, but a leader whose voice possessed the power to unite them against their common oppressor —Russia. It was not the Symphony, though, but a work coupled with it on the same program—Sibelius' patriotic choral work *Song of Athens*—that electrified the audience and placed the thirty-four-year-old composer in the forefront of his country's fight for independence.

Because of this event a political significance has sometimes been mistakenly attributed to the Symphony. The dramatic score encouraged this interpretation. Actually, as Sibelius has repeatedly pointed out, the work is a self-portrait. As such it reveals a personality which, for all of its occasional resemblances to Borodin and to Tchaikowsky, is strikingly original. As Cecil Gray, the noted British critic, has said concerning this affinity with the Russians: "Sibelius starts where they left off."

GUIDE TO LISTENING

First Movement: Above a subdued rumbling of the drums, the clarinet sings a lonely melody. When it has vanished, the orchestra, as if suddenly aroused, lunges into a statement of the first passionate theme. Swelling gradually in volume and intensity, the music rises to a climax of titanic scope.

Second Movement: The outstanding characteristic of this movement is tenderness—a brooding tenderness that conjures some deep-felt memory, in turn heroic and filled with indescribable pathos. Toward the end, the music swells into a great outburst of resent-

ful vigor, but, as if weary of the effort, subsides again into its former mood.

Third Movement: Is rebellious, fast-moving,
and its second theme, which is of gentler
cast, is quickly submerged in a return to the
powerful accents of the opening.

Fourth Movement: The last movement starts
off with the statement of a broad theme
through which runs an undercurrent of
ominous expectancy. When it is done, the
orchestra murmurs darkly for a time, as if
gathering itself together. Then, making up
its mind, it plunges forward as though in a
terrific assault on some gigantic battlement.
Surging at the end, as if in final victory, the
music sweeps everything before it.

FINLANDIA

Symphonic Poem, Op. 26

FIRST PERFORMANCE: HELSINGFORS, NOVEMBER 4,
1899

Popularity and immortality do not necessarily make good bedfellows, for they are
likely to get in each other's way. It is the
little man with the small talent that offers
an easy identification. It is he who is apt to
be given a warm reception by the public at
large. But the man of genius, by definition
one who has at least one foot already in to-
morrow, is usually greeted with less fanfare.

He may even be wholly overlooked. If not, the chances are that it will be his more obvious efforts that will draw the acclaim, not his best.

In 1899, for a patriotic celebration in Finland, Sibelius wrote a series of "Tableaux of the Past." Of the numbers comprised in the Tableaux, the last, the tone poem *Finlandia* jumped its track, as it were, and sped across national boundaries to become one of the world's popular favorites.

This success had its drawbacks. It served to identify Sibelius with what Cecil Gray terms "facile and commonplace nationalism" and to retard the recognition of his more outstanding work. This is not to say that *Finlandia* is devoid of merit. Thousands of people have enjoyed it in the past; thousands more will enjoy it in the future; and the piece, in addition, is a landmark in Finland's fight for independence. But such considerations are political and personal, not musical. As music, *Finlandia* comes close to being the least among Sibelius' other orchestral works.

GUIDE TO LISTENING

The work opens with a trenchant questioning phrase, propounded by the brasses. The strings, in answer, sing in a passage ecclesiastical in feeling, as if offering a prayer. On this material the music dwells briefly before reaching a somber pronouncement sung by the lower strings to the accompaniment of pulsating brasses. This is succeeded by a triumphantly martial passage; and from here the music progresses to a climax of crashing intensity.

SYMPHONY NO. 2
In D Major, Op. 43
FIRST PERFORMANCE: HELSINGFORS, MARCH 8, 1902

Sibelius finished his first five symphonies within the span of sixteen years (1899–1915), but a decade went by before the public generally became acquainted with these works. As an indication of the time it took any of the five symphonies to gain a foothold outside of Finland, consider that our three leading orchestras in the East—in Philadelphia, New York, and Boston—among them had only twenty-six programs listing a Sibelius symphony during the twenty-five years from 1900 to 1925.

It is the more remarkable therefore that in the recent past so great a vogue should have developed for Sibelius, and so quickly, especially for the Karelian music, *The Swan of Tuonela,* and the Second Symphony, the latter a work with the intensity of an epic struggle.

GUIDE TO LISTENING

First Movement: The work opens with a brief, pulsating introduction, its mood at first pastoral, its rise in intensity very gradual. But even from the first we hear occasional premonitions of stormier things to come. Indeed, as the music unfolds, it assumes a vivid grandeur of tremendous penetrative power.

Second Movement: Starts off mysteriously—bathed, it would seem, in the pale glow of a Northern dawn. A lonely melody, sung by the bassoon, drifts languidly over the accompaniment of low-muttering plucked strings. The mood does not last. It is eventually dispelled; and the music then quickens, grows more ardent, and heaves impassionately as it attains a fervor and nobility that are intensely moving.

Third Movement: Is restless, agitated, rushing on like some bustling stream in torrents of subdued sound. Then, suddenly, everything is still; and in this stillness the voice of the oboe briefly sings a song that glows with a pale loveliness. It is gone as abruptly as it came; but we hear it once again after a resumption of the original bustle.

Fourth Movement: The opening, announced first by the strings, then by the trumpets, takes the form of a triumphant proclamation which grows increasingly exultant. And now a hush falls on the music, but soon the orchestra surges forward again—at first slowly, deliberately, but gathering momentum and finally attaining two successive climaxes of overwhelming intensity and power.

SYMPHONY NO. 5
In E-Flat Major, Op. 82
FIRST PERFORMANCE: HELSINGFORS, DECEMBER 8, 1915

It has been said that following the composition of his Third Symphony, Sibelius stepped across a whole musical era; for in his Fourth Symphony he achieved such an extraordinary degree of terseness as to suggest to many that the work was clearly in advance of its time; perhaps the greatest single piece of music of the twentieth century.

This work also came close to being Sibelius' last symphony, for its slow acceptance by the public and even by musicians made the composer hesitate. Should he or should he not go on with the creation of these monumental works? Or should he concentrate on shorter, lighter music—more profitable and easier to write?

After weighing the matter, Sibelius decided to go on. The decision was not really his, for he was impelled as if by some irresistible inward urge.

The composition of this symphony which he began in 1914 was interrupted many times. The first World War had broken out. It had cut Sibelius off from his German publishers, and from his royalties, necessitating much tedious extra work, to earn some money; involving, too, the writing of many shorter works. But through it all Sibelius patiently carried the slowly evolving work in his mind. He remained hopeful, unperturbed, and this robust optimism was reflected with particular radiance in the sunny good humor of the Symphony. The day it was first performed, coinciding with the composer's fiftieth birthday, was celebrated in Finland as a national holiday.

GUIDE TO LISTENING

First Movement: Opens in a mood of reserve, the opening melody voiced by the French horns and supplemented by a flickering in the woodwinds. But soon the whole orchestra bestirs itself, and the music thereupon grows more agitated, moving forward with the power of a mighty wind sweeping across some great plain.

Second Movement: Starts meditatively with gentle harmonies in clarinets, bassoons, and horns through which is soon heard a characteristic figure in plucked violas and 'cellos. With this for a background, the flutes intone a slender, lonely little melody which is varied and amplified with great expressive skill.

Third Movement: Begins with an agitated passage in the strings. The music gradually swells in volume; and now, coming at us through this great curtain of sound, the French horns proclaim the majestic chief theme of the movement—a theme broad, elemental, somehow suggestive of the very core of existence, and also one of the greatest in all symphonic music. Having given it utterance, the orchestra seems to relax, catching its breath, as it were, in the statement of a second theme. Soon however it goes back to the chief theme and, gathering strength as it goes along, proclaims it with a majestic splendor that keeps broadening until its intensity is such that it seems impossible for it to become any greater. At this precise moment the Symphony ends with several widely spaced, unforgettable, crashing chords.

Friedrich Smetana

BORN 1824 AT LEITOMISCHL, Bohemia, the son
of a brewer. At five played the piano and
violin. Attended German school in Prague
where later had a job teaching. At thirty,
already known as a composer, moved to
Sweden where he fared well. Subsequently
settled in his native land as conductor of the
Opera in Prague. Overwork, resulting in illness and total deafness, led in 1883 to complete mental breakdown. Died 1884 (aged
60) in an insane asylum in Prague. Is remembered as the father of Czech music.

Smetana's music is intensely national. It
paints Bohemia in all of its aspects—its
meadows and deep forests, its streams and its
rough, jovial village life, its castles and its
legendary past. Often this music has the
boisterous ring of peasant humor; often it is
poetic and extremely moving. (For other
works by the composer see *Recommended
Recordings*.)

THE MOLDAU
Symphonic Poem from the Cycle *My Country*
FIRST PERFORMANCE: ZOFIN, APRIL 4, 1874

Smetana was a patriot, oppressed by a constant realization of his country's plight as a vassal of Austria. Not a political or military leader, but a musician, it is through music that he led his people, quickening in them a realization of their national kinship, preparing them for the day of their independence.

From this burning impulse to see his country free sprang Smetana's cycle of six symphonic poems, *My Country,* glorifying the beauty and legendary past of his native Bohemia. *The Moldau* is the second of the series, written when the composer was already stone deaf. Smetana's own interpretation of the music follows in abridged translation:

GUIDE TO LISTENING

"Two springs joyously gush in a Bohemian forest . . . sparkling in the morning sun . . . unite in the waters of a forest brook which speeds on and on. The brook becomes a

river, the Moldau . . . which swells into a
mighty stream as it flows through Bohemia's
valleys . . . through woods . . . and through
pastures, grass-grown and joyous . . . through
cataracts, foaming as it passes the rapids. . . .
A broad river now, it flows majestically into
Prague . . . finally vanishes from the poet's
gaze in the distance beyond."

French Horn

Johann Strauss, 1st and 2nd

STRAUSS, JOHANN, 1ST—"Father of the Waltz"
—was born 1804 at Vienna, the son of the
proprietor of a dance hall. At fifteen joined
a popular orchestra, playing the viola, and
at twenty-one began writing waltzes and pol-
kas whose melodic freshness and brightness
at once captivated the public. At twenty-
nine formed his own orchestra with which he
toured Europe. Died 1849 (aged 45) in Vienna.

Strauss, Johann, 2nd, son of above men-
tioned, nicknamed "The Waltz King," was
born in 1825 in Vienna. He composed his
first waltz at six but had to study music
secretly, against his father's wishes. At nineteen he formed his own orchestra, which he
conducted. Meantime his waltzes, of which
he wrote nearly four hundred, had become
national events in Austria, eclipsing in verve
and sparkle even those of his father. In
1855, world famous, he was invited to conduct
summer concerts at St. Petersburg, Russia;

and, in 1872, he gave several concerts in Boston and New York where he was acclaimed. Toward the end of his career wrote *Die Fledermaus* and other famous light operas. When he died in Vienna in 1899 (aged 73) he was mourned by the whole world and was buried next to Brahms.

"ON THE BEAUTIFUL BLUE DANUBE"

Waltzes, Op. 314

BY JOHANN STRAUSS, 2ND

FIRST PERFORMANCE: VIENNA, FEBRUARY 13, 1867

In 1867 the new director of the Viennese Men's Choral Society asked Strauss to compose a choral waltz for the Society, something bubbling over, carnival in spirit. Strauss complied.

He wrote a group of five interconnected waltzes, preceded by an introduction and followed by a concluding section leading to a rousing finish. He called it *On the Beautiful Blue Danube* and submitted it to the Society whose one hundred fifty male voices, added to the orchestra, gave the work its initial performance. Vienna, however, cannot be credited with realizing the potentialities of the piece, for the Waltz did not get started as a world-wide success until it was played at the Paris World Exhibition a few months later.

Strauss, incidentally, did not invent the title *On the Beautiful Blue Danube*. He derived it from the last line of a poem that was then running through his head. He liked the line and used it, although he must have known that the Danube, though sometimes gray or even green, is never blue.

Bassoon

Richard Strauss

BORN 1864 AT MUNICH, Germany, the son of
an accomplished player of the French horn.
Unusually precocious, he started composing
at five and, at sixteen, wrote a symphony.
It was performed while he was in college
which he soon left to become assistant to the
famous conductor, von Bülow. Up to this
point Strauss had followed conventional lines
in composition, but in his twenties, he veered
from the traditional and quickly became the
leading modernist of his time. In 1894 he
married the singer Pauline de Ahna and
went to live in Berlin. Soon after the turn
of the century, his creative faculties on the
decline, he found himself outdistanced by
other composers; eventually, almost ignored
as an important factor in modern music. In
the 1930's he moved to Vienna where he
continued his musical activities in spite of
his advancing years.

Strauss' music, though sometimes artificial

and sensational, is often brilliantly vital, witty, movingly expressive. Undoubtedly it is these latter qualities which give to it such a continued hold on the affections of the music loving public.

DON JUAN
Symphonic Poem, Op. 20
FIRST PERFORMANCE: WEIMAR, NOVEMBER 1, 1889

Don Juan was one of Strauss' first departures from the path of tradition. Up to this time he had been the white-haired boy in music, and the academicians were already dusting off appropriate adjectives with which to proclaim him as the successor of Wagner. At this point Strauss unleashed a storm of controversy and recrimination by producing a series of works which were characterized as "shocking musical audacities."

When *Don Juan* appeared, it was at once successful with the public, but its unorthodox style and "modernity" were raked over the coals. One critic even called it just a "tumult of dazzling color daubs . . ." This "tumult" has since become one of Strauss' best liked compositions.

In this work Strauss was inspired by a poem of Lenau in which this Hungarian writer takes a philosophical view of Don Juan, interpreting the amorous adventures of the famous lover not as those of a libertine but as those of a man seeking the ideal woman whom he never finds.

GUIDE TO LISTENING

The work opens energetically—its first, fiery theme, which is that of desire, leading to a flowing melody depicting the object of Don Juan's desire. We are appraised of each new conquest—of which there are several, all different in approach and mood—by a characteristic scale figure in clarinet and bassoon, following which the music grows turgid as if to suggest the Don's state of satiety and boredom. Toward the end, disappointed in his quest, the amorous knight in disgust picks a quarrel and is killed fighting a duel. A sudden pause, succeeded by mournful harmonies, announces his death.

DEATH AND TRANSFIGURATION
Symphonic Poem, Op. 24
FIRST PERFORMANCE: EISENACH, JUNE 21, 1890

Strauss is said to have written this work after an illness which almost cost him his life. In the music, which he composed when

he recovered, he attempted to render some
of the emotions he had experienced during
his illness. After the work was completed,
Alexander Ritter wrote a poetic interpretation of the music, and this poem, dealing
with a sick man's struggle with death as he
lies delirious in a garret, was approved by
Strauss and later attached to the score.

GUIDE TO LISTENING

The work opens softly with a darkly solemn theme which stands for the sick man's
"struggle with death." It is succeeded by an
impassioned second theme depicting his "desire to live." Visions of his entire life rush
through the delirious brain of the sick man
—visions of striving yet never attaining; of
joy and fleeting happiness, but also of frustration and sorrow. As the liberating hand
of Death finally frees his soul from its earthly
cares, the music rises and broadens rejoicingly
in an apotheosis of deliverance, of Transfiguration.

TILL EULENSPIEGEL'S MERRY PRANKS
Symphonic Poem, Op. 28
FIRST PERFORMANCE: COLOGNE, NOVEMBER 5,
1895

Till Eulenspiegel is the name of a legendary

rogue whose clever wit and inexhaustible bag of tricks, personifying as they do the triumph of the nimble wit over the more sedate virtues of a day-by-day world, have been the fascination of every German schoolboy for many generations. And, judging from the music, Strauss must have found himself in his element while writing a good part of it. For at no time did he succeed so well in injecting humor into music as when he undertook to portray in sound Till Eulenspiegel's many vidid escapades: the rogue's brazen gallop on horseback through the market place, overturning carts with flowers, fish, and vegetables; his shameless impersonation of a clergyman; his eventual capture and hanging at the hands of the authorities.

GUIDE TO LISTENING

Claude Debussy who thoroughly enjoyed *Till Eulenspiegel* but was not quite sure whether he approved of it or not, said of the music:

"Listening to the piece was like an hour at the asylum;—distracted clarinets described strange curves; muted trumpets remained muted; and the horns, as if anticipating a sneeze, hurried to say: 'God bless you!' while the big drum thundered 'boom-boom' underscoring the clown's every kick and gesture.

Hearing it all you burst out laughing or howled in agony, and when it was all over you were amazed to find things in their normal place."

Cello

Igor Stravinsky

BORN 1882 NEAR ST. PETERSBURG, Russia, the
son of an opera singer. Began composing
early though preparing for a legal career. At
twenty-five, with a symphony to his credit,
became a private pupil of Rimsky-Korsakoff.
Two years later, a meeting with Diaghileff,
dynamic impressario of the Ballets Russes in
Paris, led in quick succession (1910–13) to
the composition of three ballets—*The Fire
Bird, Petrouchka, The Rite of Spring*—which
established Stravinsky as one of the most
striking musical innovators of his time.
During subsequent years lived quietly in
France, becoming a French citizen and tend-
ing increasingly toward a neo-classic style
more in the spirit of the older masters.

Stravinsky's music charms with its variety
of scintillating tonal color; it startles with its
rowdy vigor and its garish glare; it also thrills
with its pulsating, elemental force and its

great heaving, pagan rhythms. It is music with a thrust—relentlessly unmindful of convention, at times blithely cacophonous, yet always intensely alive.

For other works by the composer, see *Recommended Recordings*.)

THE FIRE BIRD
Orchestral Suite Drawn from the Ballet, Similarly Named
FIRST PERFORMED: PARIS, JUNE 25, 1910

In 1909, still in his twenties and still largely unknown, Stravinsky received a telegram from the incredible Diaghileff. The telegram was brief and to the point. In it the impressario asked if Mr. Stravinsky would undertake the writing of the music for a ballet on the Russian fairy-tale subject, *The Fire Bird.* The thing had to be done in short order—conceived, scored, and rehearsed in a few months.

Stravinsky accepted, but not without some hesitation; and we are left to wonder what would have happened if he had refused. For it was with *The Fire Bird* that the great vogue for Stravinsky's music began to spread throughout the world.

The story of the Fire Bird tells of the capture of this gleaming bird with jewel-like eyes, by the young Prince Ivan Tsarevich. Yielding to the Bird's entreaties, he releases it and is rewarded with a magic feather which enables him to destroy the wicked ogre Kastchei and win the hand of a beautiful Princess.

GUIDE TO LISTENING

Introduction and Dance of the Fire Bird: The orchestra murmurs mysteriously as it paints a picture of the gorgeous orchard where the Fire Bird dwells. To the accompaniment of glistening tonal cascades, the wondrous creature appears and executes a dance. Swift darts of sound herald the appearance of the Prince as he springs at the Bird. The Fire Bird cries out, entreats, and the Prince lets it go.

Dance of the Princesses: Awakening from a deep sleep, the Prince finds himself at the foot of a crumbling castle from whose gates issue thirteen Princesses. Two flutes picture their stately procession, and we catch tonal glimpses of their loveliness as they begin to dance. The eyes of the Prince are on the thirteenth Princess—the loveliest of all.

Dance of Kastchei, Berseuse, and Finale: Made bold by love, Prince Ivan flings open the gates of the castle, releasing Kastchei's prisoners. A sharp, metallic crash in the orchestra signalizes the appearance of the ogre. He chases the Prince, but the latter wards off the monster with the magic feather and, to protect the thirteenth Princess, casts a spell over her. To the accompaniment of gently caressing music she falls asleep. The young Prince, who has meantime conquered the ogre, awakens the Princess, and the two gaze rapturously into each other's eyes.

PETROUCHKA
Orchestral Suite Drawn from the Ballet, Similarly Named
FIRST PERFORMED: PARIS, JUNE 13, 1911

The music for the ballet *Petrouchka* was begun soon after the production of *The Fire Bird*—"to refresh myself," as Stravinsky puts it, before shouldering weightier composing problems. Its performance served to clinch the composer's international reputation—and no wonder; for it is salty music with a street-song quality and a robust freshness that have so far successfully withstood the test of time.

Petrouchka is a familiar "sight" at every Russian country fair. He is a puppet in a marionette show—a symbolic figure—always struggling, pathetically and comically, against a fate he cannot master.

Igor Stravinsky

First tableau: The scene is a Russian country fair, colorful and noisy. Boisterous crowds mill around. An organ grinder is heard briefly; a magician starts playing the flute. Suddenly a hush falls over the crowd. The curtain of the little theatre is jerked up, revealing three puppets: Petrouchka, the Ballerina, and the Moor. All three break into a Russian dance. The curtain goes down with a thump.

Second tableau: The curtain goes up. Petrouchka is propelled on the stage. He jerks himself up, and his lamentations are picked up by the piano and blared forth by the brasses. Soon the Ballerina enters. To attract her attention Petrouchka capers about, but she will have none of him.

Third tableau: The curtain goes up—in the Moor's room. The atmosphere is ominous. The clarinets intone a low melody as the Moor dances. Enters the Ballerina, playing a brazen little tune on the cornet. She flirts with the Moor and dances a waltz with him. When Petrouchka appears, interrupting their lovemaking, the Moor chases him and trounces him soundly.

Fourth tableau: Again we hear the familiar noises of the fair. It is evening. The crowd watches the dance of the Nursemaids. Following a low groan in the orchestra, a peasant appears with a tame bear on a chain. The beast dances awkwardly while his master pipes a foolish little tune. Two other dances follow: the vigorous tripping of the Coachmen and Grooms, and the dance of the Masks in which the whole crowd presently joins. Suddenly Petrouchka appears, pursued by the Moor who fells him with a blow of his saber. The magician tries to reassure everyone, explaining that these are but puppets. Slowly, the crowd disperses. Overhead, Petrouchka's ghost waves menacingly at the Moor.

THE RITE OF SPRING (SACRE DU PRINTEMPS)

Originally Composed as a Ballet, Similarly Named

FIRST PERFORMANCE: PARIS, MAY 29, 1913

Probably the greatest virtue of Stravinsky's music is its remarkable aptness to the subject which inspired it. If, for instance, it attempts to give a musical impression of an emerald-eyed, glistening Fire Bird that dwells in an enchanted orchard, the tone picture it draws makes us all but physically aware of the Bird's presence. If it attempts to sketch

[201]

Igor Stravinsky

a gaudy and bustling country fair, it succeeds so well that we seem, for the moment, to be transported to the very midst of the jostling carnival crowd. When, on the other hand, it undertakes to depict so powerful a subject as the worship of the forces of Nature by primitive man, it is just as realistic, sparing us nothing—like it or not—and on first hearing we may not like it—at all.

This at least was the reaction of the usually well-behaved, fashionable Paris audience that gathered in 1913 to witness the first performance of the ballet *The Rite of Spring*. What happened made musical history. Murmurs were heard even as the piece started, and soon bedlam broke loose. Excitement ran high. People whistled. They rose up from their seats to insult the performers and denounce the composer. Others engaged in fist fights, shouting their disapproval. Stravinsky, the conductor, and the performers were in a frenzy, but the performance somehow was carried through. When it was over, everyone was exhausted, including the audience. Powerful music, this.

Today audiences no longer riot when confronted with the work. They come prepared to listen to a musical landmark, expecting to be shocked, and they are usually not disappointed. The work still has great power although its impact is probably not so overwhelming, even on first hearing, as it undoubtedly must have been in 1913.

Although as a ballet *The Rite of Spring* is subdivided into two parts—the first, dealing with primitive man's mystical adoration of the Earth; and the second, with the sacrifice of a virgin to promote fertility—in concert, these two parts are played without a break.

GUIDE TO LISTENING

1) *Adoration of the Earth:* The work opens with the bassoon, way up in its high register, its haltingly plaintive voice visioning "the mystery of the physical world in Spring." Other wind instruments join in, intensifying the mysterious vernal mood, and (as the curtain rises) we witness a bleak valley dominated by immense boulders, with a group of men at the right and a group of maidens at the left. The maidens rise, one by one, and join in a sharply undulating ritual dance. There is a brief pause, but the tenseness increases. The men now rouse themselves and begin to dance, stamping the ground to the accompaniment of a relentless chord in the strings, repeated vehemently, over and over. (This chord, perhaps, has sent more chills

down people's spines than any other single passage in music, unless it be the Sacrificial Dance—see below.)

The music quickens as the youths and maidens stage a mock abduction—a part of the ritual. After several more dances—one of them the languorous, mysterious Vernal Dance —the music rises to a furious climax while the tubas ponderously announce the appearance of the Sage, oldest member of the tribe. There is a momentary hush. The Sage prostrates himself and blesses the soil, invoking its rejuvenation. As he rises there is sharp roll of the drums, and the youths and maidens leap to their feet in a Dance of the Earth which steadily gains in vehemence.

2) *The Sacrifice:* A brooding introduction, characterized by Edwin Evans as "gloomy with the oppression of the vast forces of Nature," opens the second part. It is followed by a dance of the maidens who move slowly to the swaying rhythms of the Mystical Circle of the Adolescents. With progressive intensity the music portrays the choice of the virgin to be offered in sacrifice, the savagely angular dance to her glorification, and finally, the Sacrificial Dance of the Chosen One—unforgettable in its mystic rapture and frenzied climax.

Deems Taylor

BORN 1885 IN NEW YORK CITY. Graduated N. Y. University expecting to become an architect. Later studied music, but took up journalistic career; first, as war correspondent in France; later, as music critic in U. S. As a composer, gained recognition through several orchestral works and the operas *The King's Henchman* and *Peter Ibbetson*. Lately, achieved further prominence through his books and his comments on music during Sunday broadcast of the N. Y. Philharmonic Orchestra.

THROUGH THE LOOKING GLASS
Suite for Orchestra, Op. 12
FIRST PERFORMANCE: NEW YORK, FEBRUARY 18, 1921

In the gentle, half-mocking detachment of Carroll's imaginative poem, Deems Taylor found a perfect counterpart to his own musical temperament. But Alice's homeland thought differently. British critics, perhaps a little resentful at this act of "trespassing" by an American, sniffed at the Suite, referred to its composer as "a good musician, no doubt, but far from catching the white rabbit." To make up for this, in the U. S., the piece was an immediate success.

GUIDE TO LISTENING

Dedication: A wistfully tender song captures the spirit of the poem's opening stanza in which Carroll bids children join him in the fairy-tale journey he is about to relate.

Garden of Flowers: Alice passes through the looking glass and finds herself in a beautiful garden where the flowers wave to her and chatter gaily.

Jabberwocky: After the fearsome opening theme, portraying Jabberwocky, the monster (the word puzzled Alice), the clarinet intones Humpty-Dumpty's explanation. The hero of the piece is pictured standing by a tree with sword unsheathed, awaiting the monster. When the latter heaves into sight, he is engaged in battle by the hero and finally slain.

Looking-Glass Insects: This episode tells of Alice's fascination on meeting these insects—a gnat, the size of a chicken; a bee which "in fact is an elephant"; and the fly that lived on "weak tea with cream in it."

The White Knight: The Knight—in his own eyes, dashing, invincible; in reality, gentle and a bit ridiculous—is portrayed by two appropriately contrasting themes. The Knight stages an exhibition for Alice—and falls off his horse. As he finally trots off and is lost around the turn, Alice waves her handkerchief.

Flute

◆◆◆◆◆◆◆◆◆◆◆◆◆◆◆◆◆◆◆◆◆◆◆◆◆◆◆◆◆◆◆◆

Peter Ilitch Tchaikowsky

BORN 1840 AT KAMSKO-VOTINSK, Russia, the son
of a mining engineer. Showed no startling
gift for music as a child and was steered
toward a civil service career. Was graduated
from law school to a government clerkship
but turned about face at twenty-three to devote himself solely to music. Within ten
years established himself as a ranking musician in his own country and was, along with
Borodin, the first of Russian composers to
win a large following abroad. Devoted himself in later years largely to composition.
Died of cholera in 1893 (aged 53) at St.
Petersburg, Russia.

Tchaikowsky's music is highly subjective,
occasionally banal, but always intense, even
poignant, in its expression of the darker,
brooding moods. In its lighter vein it can be
charming, elegant, and even sparkling, but it
seldom reaches a plane of contagious gayety
or real light-hearted merriment.

ROMEO AND JULIET
Overture-Fantasy (after Shakespeare)
FIRST PERFORMANCE: MOSCOW, MARCH 16, 1870

Tchaikowsky was twenty-eight when he fell madly in love with the famous and alluring French singer, Desirée Artot. The time was December 1868, and during that month the young composer was radiantly happy. His happiness was brief. Soon he was sitting in a concert hall with tears streaming down his face as he listened to Mademoiselle Artot. The singer had just returned from Warsaw where, without warning, she had married the popular baritone Mariano Padilla.

To this unhappy experience, rightly or wrongly, has been attributed some of the poignant almost rhapsodic eloquence of the *Romeo and Juliet* music.

GUIDE TO LISTENING

(1) The introductory passage is solemn in character, projecting the figure of Friar Lawrence through softly voiced liturgical harmonies, entrusted to clarinets and bassoons. After an ominously subdued passage,

(2) the music quickens, characterizing the conflict of the opposing houses; becomes

more and more tempestuous. When it subsides,

(3) a song-like melody emerges. What we hear is the English horn and muted violas voicing Romeo's rhapsodic cry: "Oh, starry night of ecstasy!" With each repetition this poignantly beautiful melody grows in eloquence and ardor. But soon

(4) the strife music returns, rising to a climax of tumultuous fury. After a soft succession of chords, Romeo's song rises for the last time in a dirge-like lament. The music ends with an ominous roll of the drums and a few crashing chords.

CONCERTO (PIANO AND ORCHESTRA) NO. 1
In B-Flat Minor, Op. 23
FIRST PERFORMANCE: BOSTON, OCTOBER 25, 1875

When Tchaikowsky finished this Piano Concerto—his first—he dedicated it to Nicholas Rubinstein and asked that eminent musician, whom he regarded as his friend, to listen to a piano rendition of the composition. What happened is vividly recorded in Tchaikowsky's own words:

"I played the first movement. Not a single word, not even a comment. If you could only know how intolerably foolish one feels when one sets before a friend a dish of one's own making, and the friend eats it—and says nothing. . . . At least say something! Find fault if you wish, in a friendly way, but for heaven's sake speak out—utter a sympathetic word even if you can't offer praise. . . .

"I took patience and played the piece through. Silence again. 'Well?' I said as I rose from the piano. Then there came gushing from Rubinstein's mouth a veritable torrent of words. . . . It appeared that my Concerto was worthless, absolutely unplayable. . . ."

Stung to the quick by this explosive rejection, Tchaikowsky promptly erased the original inscription and re-dedicated his Concerto to von Bülow, famous German conductor, who took the composition to America and played it in its initial performance with the Boston Symphony.

GUIDE TO LISTENING

First Movement: The Concerto opens with a majestic theme given out stentorian-fashion by all four French horns against a crashing orchestra. The piano now enters, sweeping with chords across the keyboard. It takes over the melody which it elaborates, alternating with the orchestra. Presently there appears a second theme which is brisk and skipping. (We learn from the composer that he heard a blind beggar at a country fair singing this impudent little tune.)

Second Movement: Begins with a tender, lull-aby-like melody, given out first by the flute, accompanied by plucked, muted strings, then by the piano playing gently and softly. In the middle of the movement, after some jerky by-play on the piano, there appears a saucy waltz tune (which, we are told, the composer picked up in a dance hall).

Third Movement: Begins after a brief intro-duction with a boisterous dance tune—peas-ant-like and very Russian. The Concerto ends on a vigorous note.

SYMPHONY NO. 4
In F Minor, Op. 36
FIRST PERFORMANCE: MOSCOW, FEBRUARY 22, 1878

During the years 1876–78 two women crossed Tchaikowsky's path, affecting his life so profoundly that the emotional echoes of their presence, fairly permeate the Fourth Symphony which he was then creating.

The first was a young woman whom the composer married out of an exaggerated and, as it turned out, a pretty ruinous sense of chivalry. The wedding took place in the summer of 1877, but the marriage went on the rocks within two months, leaving the composer a nervous wreck.

The other woman was his senior by nine years, a widow, Madame von Meck. She was a music lover, an admirer of Tchaikowsky's music. Inquiries as to his circumstances revealed to her that he was in financial difficulties. There followed an exchange of letters. Then, during the year 1877, Madame von Meck decided to help Tchaikowsky by supplying him with an annual allowance of $3000. The only condition she exacted was that he never seek to meet her. Tchaikowsky's acceptance led to the development of one of the strangest relationships on record, carried on entirely by mail—the composer drawing his inspiration from this woman he had never met and pouring out his soul to her in frequent, detailed, and eloquent letters.

It is to Madame von Meck that he dedicated his Fourth Symphony, a work revealing a mature Tchaikowsky at his heroic best. The composer's own interpretation of the music follows in abridged form:

GUIDE TO LISTENING

First Movement: "The introduction," writes Tchaikowsky, "is the kernel of the whole

[213]

symphony." (*This refers to the opening—sharply menacing, chilling, phrase uttered by French horns and bassoons.*) "It stands for destiny—that fateful force which keeps the impulse toward happiness from ever being fully realized. . . . This force cannot be evaded. . . . Perforce one must submit, lamenting inwardly. . . ." (*Here the violas and 'cellos intone the symphony's first, graceful theme*) following which the music, in turn tender, compassionate, and brooding, progresses to its end where the relentless warning phrase which opened the Symphony is stridently repeated.

Second Movement: ". . . expresses a different phase of sadness." (*Here we hear the oboe's plaintive voice in a plain little melody—very Russian, very lonely.*) "It is that feeling of fleeting melancholy which comes to him who sits alone of an evening, tired from the day's work. . . ."

Third Movement: ". . . expresses the flights of quickened fancy." (*Passage for plucked strings*) "In this mood, exhilarated slightly by wine . . . one feels neither sadness nor gayety. . . ."

Fourth Movement: "If thou canst find happiness in thyself, look for it in others." (*Following a vehement outburst from the orchestra, the woodwinds take up a Russian folk tune—sad yet persuasive.*) "Go to the people. Observe how others find their joy. . . . Partake of their merriment . . . but no! No sooner hast thou been drawn away from thyself than unrelenting fate appears again. . . ." (*Here the fate theme returns*) ". . . Disregard it! See how merry others can be. . . . Rejoice in their happiness! Life will not be unbearable if you do."

1812: OUVERTURE SOLENELLE
Op. 49
FIRST PERFORMANCE: MOSCOW, AUGUST 20, 1882

When Tchaikowsky's publisher suggested to the composer that he write this overture to order for the celebration to be held in the great Kremlin square, commemorating the Russian victory of 1812 that checked Napoleon's invasion, Tchaikowsky answered curtly that he was not a "concocter of festival pieces." In this he was probably right, for though he later relented and wrote the Overture, he always remained a bit self-conscious about it.

Whether his memory of this work was perhaps a trifle jarred by the alleged suggestion that he substitute a company of artillery for the bass drum in the initial performance; or whether he realized that the piece turned out

just a bit too sensational and noisy to do him
much credit—whatever the reasons, it has
been said that Tchaikowsky usually avoided
the subject, dismissing the Overture as of
"purely local and patriotic significance."

GUIDE TO LISTENING

The work opens with the strains of a familiar Russian prayer: "God Preserve Thy People." The prayer is elaborated and leads to
an animated passage which becomes increasingly martial in character. We distinguish echoes of the Marseillaise. This is
followed by a melody based on a Russian
folk tune. Thereupon the Marseillaise returns. It leads, at the close of the piece, first
to a crashing reiteration of the prayer, and,
finally, to a thunderous proclamation of the
Russian National Anthem.

SYMPHONY NO. 5
In E Minor, Op. 65
FIRST PERFORMANCE: ST. PETERSBURG, NOVEM-
BER 5, 1888

Fortunate it is that music has never had to
depend for its survival on the opinion held
by composers of each other's work. If it had,

very little music of the past would have
reached us today—certainly not the music of
Tchaikowsky or Brahms. For Tchaikowsky
could not abide Brahms whose work he described as "cold," "obscure," "full of preten-
sions," and "boring." And Brahms apparently reciprocated by bluntly informing
Tchaikowsky that the latter's Fifth Symphony,
in his opinion, did not amount to much.

This must have been especially vexing to
the composer because he had himself come to
entertain misgivings on the merits of the
Symphony after the Russian press had ignored it and the first three performances had
not been a success. In a letter to a friend,
Tchaikowsky even went so far as to declare
his Symphony "patchy" and "insincere." He
had of course no way of knowing that this
work was destined to become one of a half-
dozen of the greatest symphonic favorites of
the Western World.

GUIDE TO LISTENING

First Movement: Two clarinets open the
Symphony with a melody in which we find
the inner message of the entire work. For
this somber, Slavic tune, reappears in all four
movements of the Symphony. After an ominous slackening of pace, we hear the principal

theme of the movement—a melody which seems but a quickened echo of the gloomy Slavic tune.

Second Movement: The melody that emerges shortly after the opening of this movement is the delight of most players of the French horn, for it provides an opportunity for sustained solo playing. This melody is infinitely, almost cloyingly, lovely, and the mood changes only slightly when we reach the brief contrasting melody.

Third Movement: A dainty waltz—cheerful yet never really gay—occupies most of this movement.

Fourth Movement: The movement opens solemnly, with the now familiar Slavic melody. By degrees, working its way through various developments—some sad and others joyous, we finally reach an ominous pause, and hear the Slavic melody again, but stated boldly, almost with exultation, sweeping us through to a triumphant end.

NUTCRACKER SUITE

Op. 71-A—from the Fairy Ballet *Casse-Noisette*

FIRST PERFORMANCE: ST. PETERSBURG, MARCH 19, 1892

Early in 1891, Tchaikowsky was commissioned to write a ballet for the Imperial Opera in St. Petersburg. Though none too pleased, for he was then in the throes of composing his opera *The Queen of Spades*, Tchaikowsky set to work and completed most of the first act before leaving Russia to fulfil an engagement that took him to Paris and New York.

An incident that occurred during this trip quickened his interest in the ballet. Wandering down a side street in Paris, so the story goes, Tchaikowsky heard, coming from an open window, beautiful musical sounds, such as he had never heard before. Investigation uncovered an entirely new musical instrument, the celesta, never before heard in public for it had recently been invented by a Frenchman.

So captivated was Tchaikowsky by this "diminutive looking piano" and its silvery tones, that he decided to introduce it to the world by assigning to it a place of honor in his Nutcracker ballet. This ballet is based on the following Hoffman fairy tale:

A little girl, Marie, receives a nutcracker as a Christmas gift. During the night, stealing downstairs to see her new toy, she is overtaken by a troupe of mice. Thereupon the nutcracker and all the other toys in the room come to life. In the course of the battle that ensues, the nutcracker is almost killed, but, rescued by Marie, is transformed into a young prince, and he and Marie fly off together to the kingdom of the Sugar Plum Fairy.

GUIDE TO LISTENING

1) *Overture Miniature:* This determined little tune, played by the strings and woodwinds, serves as an introduction to the Suite.

2) *March:* Suggestive of a procession of dolls is this sprightly march in which the clarinets, French horns, and trumpets are strongly in evidence.

3) *Dance of the Sugar Plum Fairy:* Here the celesta is heard following a brief introductory passage in plucked strings. The appearance of the instrument cannot be missed, for it speaks in a voice almost as sugary as that of the Sugar Plum Fairy herself.

4) *Trepak:* This vigorous Russian folk dance prepares us for the sharp change of mood in the dance that is to follow.

5) *Arab Dance:* The clarinets, followed by the strings, execute a dreamy, drone-like dance, suggestive of Bagdad or Cairo.

6) *Chinese Dance:* Supported by bassoons and double basses, the flutes sally in a sprightly tune vaguely Chinese in flavor.

7) *Dance of the Mirlitons:* Three flutes supported by strings are most prominent in this charming little piece.

8) *Waltz of the Flowers:* A short introduction comprising several runs on the harp introduces this captivating waltz whose lilting rhythms pull you right out of your chair, rivaling anything penned by Johann Strauss himself.

SYMPHONY NO. 6
In B Minor, Op. 74 (*Pathetique*)
FIRST PERFORMANCE: ST. PETERSBURG, OCTOBER 16, 1893

Into this work the Russian composer seems to have poured all that was darkest in his heart—despair, and misery, and the crushing finality of human destiny as manifested through death.

The Pathetique Symphony was at once Tchaikowsky's greatest creative effort—and his swan song. Four days after its initial performance the composer drank a glass of water, drawn from the tap. Less than a week later he had died of cholera.

GUIDE TO LISTENING

First Movement: A bassoon, its voice issuing from the cavernous depths of its lower register, starts us off on our journey of frustration and pain. This is but a fragment split off from the first theme which presently bursts forth on us in an urgent cry uttered by the strings. The music surges to a climax, then slackens, and after a brief pause reaches the second theme—a melody expressive of a calmer mood, as if of resignation. The tragic passages that follow are among the best ever to flow from Tchaikowsky's pen.

Second Movement: The charming melody of graceful contour that runs through a large part of this movement is something of a rarity —a waltz yet not a waltz—for it is written in 5⁄4 time. There follows a second melody— less troubled, somehow more pensive.

Third Movement: The passage in the strings with which this movement opens—a passage that is agitated, incessantly busy, broken into by occasional snatches of a martial character —leads us by degrees into a march of gigantic proportions and of fierce, irresistible forward sweep.

Fourth Movement: This movement, almost funereal in character, contains what is probably Tchaikowsky's most eloquent music. The anguished lament of its opening is a cry of utter despair; the second, contrasting theme which follows immediately, flowing heavily like the murky waters of a great stream, is a sob of abject resignation.

Richard Wagner

BORN 1813 AT LEIPZIG, Germany, the son of a police official. Industrious at school, he translated Homer's *Odyssey* from Greek to German at thirteen. A little later he wrote a dramatic work of his own, *Leubald*, which, after hearing Beethoven's Overture to Goethe's *Egmont*, he attempted to set to music. Not until he was past eighteen, however, did he undertake a serious study of music. Yet he was soon turning out operas and even a symphony, and at twenty-one he became a conductor.

When twenty-three he married the actress Wilhelmine Planer and with her went the following year as conductor to Riga. It was there that he decided to become a dramatic composer. This decision took him to Paris where, instead of the opportunities hoped for, he encountered poverty and rebuff. Acceptance and performance in 1842 of his opera *Rienzi* brought him back to Germany where he became a conductor in Dresden. It was there that he began his literary labors on the "Ring."

Already well known as a composer, he was forced to leave Germany in 1849 for political reasons. Thereafter, while living in different countries in Europe, he composed and conducted but was harassed for lack of money until 1863 when his financial worries were lifted by the timely intervention of the young King of Bavaria, whose encouragement and help was at this point decisive in Wagner's career. At fifty-seven married the divorced Cosima von Bülow, daughter of Liszt, and, at sixty-three, now the unchallenged superman of music, knew the triumph of having the whole cycle of music dramas, *Der Ring des Nibelungen,* produced in a theater at Beuruth specially constructed for the purpose. Died 1883 (aged 69) of a heart attack at Venice, Italy.

Wagner's music, like Wagner's other projects, such as his literary undertakings, has a towering quality all its own. Sometimes it is a little crushing in its weight, but at its best this music is capable of remarkable power and lyric intensity. Above all it somehow always conveys a sense of the powerful personality that lies behind its creation—the indomitable spirit of the man who, having decided to supplant what he considered an out-

worn artistic form (the opera) with something new and vitally alive (the music
drama) applied himself to this task single-
handed and achieved his goal through the
exercise of stupendous effort and determina-
tion.

OVERTURE TO "THE FLYING DUTCHMAN"

FIRST PERFORMANCE OF THE OPERA: DRESDEN,
JANUARY 2, 1843

In 1839, Wagner who was conducting in
Riga, decided to become a dramatic composer. That summer, together with his wife,
he left for Paris via England. The trip from
Libau to London was very rough, but it was
this stormy voyage on the sea which provided
Wagner with the impulse and inspiration for
the composition of his fifth opera, *The Flying
Dutchman.*

The plot of this opera deals with the plight
of a ghost ship and its ghost captain, The
Flying Dutchman, who is cursed with having
forever to roam the seas unless he can find a
wife who will be faithful to him unto death.
Chancing during a storm upon the ship of
the sea-captain Daland, he induces this worthy
mariner to give his daughter, Senta, to him

in marriage. The interference of Erik, who
loves Senta, thwarts this plan, but the girl,
who has meanwhile fallen in love with the
mysterious stranger, throws herself into the
sea and drowns, thus releasing the soul of The
Flying Dutchman from its bondage to this
world.

GUIDE TO LISTENING

From the very opening of the Overture, the
vision of a stormy sea dominates the music.
Through this tumult of wind and raging
water are heard suggestions of the broad
theme of the doomed Dutchman. There is a
brief lull, as if he were dreaming of salvation,
but the tumult is soon resumed. The music
ends in the triumphant accents of the re-
demption theme.

OVERTURE TO "TANNHÄUSER"

FIRST PERFORMANCE OF THE OPERA: DRESDEN,
OCTOBER 19, 1845

The two and a half years which Wagner
spent in Paris, seeking his fortune as a dramatic composer, proved disappointing. He
was turned down at the Opera and was barely
able to scrape enough money together to pay

for life's necessities by arranging music and writing songs and articles.

His stay in Paris had one good result. It made him realize that he was German to the core and led him back to Beethoven and von Weber whose music he had neglected, with salutary effects immediately noticeable in his own composition. Finally, it brought him back to Germany, where he unquestionably belonged; and it was then that he started working on a new opera, *Der Venusberg,* later renamed *Tannhäuser.*

The plot of this opera deals with the sad tale of the Minstrel Knight Tannhäuser who, though engaged to the lovely Elisabeth, niece of the ruling Prince, strays to the magic grotto in the Thuringian mountains where he falls under the spell of the beautiful Goddess of Love, Venus. For his adoration of the heathen Goddess, Tannhäuser is sentenced to travel with a group of pilgrims to seek the forgiveness of the Pope in Rome. Several months later the pilgrims return without Tannhäuser from whom the Pope has withheld his forgiveness. Thereupon Elisabeth breathes her last. During her funeral the haggard Tannhäuser returns, and, as he reappears, the news is brought that he has been forgiven.

Richard Wagner

GUIDE TO LISTENING

The Overture starts off with the Pilgrims' Chant which draws near, passes, and is lost in the distance. And now, at nightfall, we are transported to the magic mountain, Venusberg, in Thuringia. Here Tannhäuser sounds his jubilant Song of Love. In answer, the Goddess Venus comes out of the mountain, bewitching the Minstrel. But a new day already is dawning. In the distance, coming closer, the Pilgrims' Chant is heard again.

PRELUDE AND "LOVE-DEATH"
From "Tristan and Isolde"
FIRST PERFORMANCE: PRELUDE: PRAGUE, MARCH 12, 1859; OPERA: MUNICH, JUNE 10, 1865

Wagner conceived the idea for the opera *Tristan and Isolde* as early as 1854, but he did not complete the work until 1859. In the intervening years he was kept busy chiefly with his cycle of music dramas *Der Ring Des Nibelungen*.

These years were stormy. Wagner's political troubles were over, for he had fled from Germany to the safety of Switzerland. His difficulties now were marital. Together with his wife he occupied a "refuge in the hills" provided by the rich merchant Wesendonk. The place was perfect for intensive work. It would have been ideal, had it not been for the explosive undercurrents in the atmosphere caused by the "situation" that had developed between his wife, Minna, and his hostess, Mathilde Wesendonk. Of the closeness of his relationship to the latter we may judge from a letter he wrote to her in 1861. In it he said: "That I composed *Tristan,* I thank you from the bottom of my being, forever and ever."

The plot of this opera deals with Tristan's love for the Princess Isolde. As the story opens, Tristan is escorting the Princess on a ship from Ireland to Cornwall following her betrothal to his uncle, King Mark. Isolde returns Tristan's love, but because he avoids her, lest his passion lead him to break his trust, she bids him share with her a parting goblet containing poison. A substitution of a love potion for the poison causes the two lovers to fall in each other's arms. Later they are betrayed and Tristan, mortally wounded in a duel, dies in Isolde's arms.

GUIDE TO LISTENING

The music opens with a quietly glowing melody—the theme of Longing—sung by the 'cellos. Gradually rising in intensity, the

music soars impassionately, then drops back
to a whisper, as it paints love's ecstatic experience.

PRELUDE TO "DIE MEISTER-SINGER"

FIRST PERFORMANCE: PRELUDE: LEIPZIG, NOVEM-
BER 1, 1862; OPERA: MUNICH, JUNE 21, 1868

A political exile for twelve years, Wagner
was allowed to return to Germany in 1860,
and it was shortly after this amnesty was
granted that the music of his great comic
opera, *Die Meistersinger,* first entered his
mind. Hearing it inwardly "with the utmost
distinctness," he "at once wrote down the
main part of the Overture." The remainder
of the opera, however, was written piecemeal
—partly in Paris, partly in Vienna and Triebschen near Lucerne. Wagner's financial difficulties kept him on the go; his ability to
push ahead with several major works at once,
made his progress on *Die Meistersinger* very
slow. When he finally completed the opera
he was just fifty-four years old and at the
peak of his creative powers.

The plot of this opera takes us to Sixteenth
Century Germany; to the city of Nurenberg
whose worthy burghers, though lovers of song,
had hedged themselves in with such pedantic

restrictions that the office of "marker" became necessary to record all the "breaches" made by the singers. During the annual singing contest of the celebrated guild of the Meister-singers—a contest offering the hand of the beautiful Eva to the victor—Walther von Stolzing, who is in love with Eva, is refused as a candidate because, though talented, he is untutored in the rules of song. However, through the clever machinations of the kindly cobbler, Hans Sachs, Walther finally wins both the contest and the hand of Eva.

GUIDE TO LISTENING

The Overture opens with a vigorous march theme which immediately transports us to Six-teenth Century Nurenberg where we mix, to quote Wagner's own words "with somewhat blunt, three-cornered folk." Indeed, the music conjures just that: three-cornered, blunt, good-humored German burghers. A second theme, which is more lyrical, is associated with Walther's and Eva's love; a pompous third theme depicts the Meistersinger guild with all its rigid regulations.

A SIEGFRIED IDYLL

FIRST PERFORMED: TRIEBSCHEN, SWITZERLAND:
DECEMBER 25, 1870

At forty Wagner met the sixteen-year-old

daughter of Liszt, Cosima. Years later he fell
in love with her, and married her after she
had divorced von Bülow. Their wedding
took place in August 1870, and that same
year, as a surprise for his wife's thirty-third
birthday which fell on Christmas day, Wagner
wrote his famous *Siegfried Idyll* in which all
the tenderness of his conjugal bliss found expression.

The piece was performed by an orchestra
which assembled on Christmas morning on
the stairs of the villa in which the Wagners
were staying; and, promptly at seven-thirty,
Wagner who had kept the whole thing a secret
from his wife, led the orchestra. Cosima,
awakening to the strains of the music, was
so moved that tears came to her eyes. For
years later she regarded the piece as somehow part of herself.

GUIDE TO LISTENING

The prevailing mood of the Idyll is peaceful tenderness. As such, the music undoubtedly reflects Wagner's feelings toward his family. At the same time, its source of inspiration lies beyond these personal feelings, for
between 1869–71 Wagner was working on his
music drama *Siegfried,* and it is interesting to
note that during that time he was so completely engrossed in and identified with his

Richard Wagner

subject that he not only named his son
"Siegfried" (born June 6, 1869) but drew
most of the material for the Idyll from the
third act of that music drama.

MAGIC FIRE MUSIC
From "Die Walküre"
FIRST PERFORMANCE OF THE OPERA: MUNICH,
JUNE 26, 1870

During the period of his conductorship in
Dresden, as far back as the early 1840's, Wagner became interested in the *Niebelungen
Ring*, that great German epic derived from
a division of the Norse Sagas known as the
Eddas. Impressed with the scope and beauty
of this mythological material, Wagner im-
mersed himself in it. He then wrote a prose
version of the "Ring" which he published in
1848.

Having obtained this initial grip on his
subject, Wagner undertook to dramatize this
material. In the course of time he molded
it into a single well-knit, well-motivated poem
which he called "Siegfried's Death." Still dis-
satisfied, he reworked the legend and achieved
greater coherence by distributing its action
among three parts which he called *Die Walküre, Siegfried,* and *Götterdämmerung.* To

this trilogy he later added another part, *Das Rheingold,* which he placed at the beginning of the cycle since it served to clarify the action portrayed in the other three works. Only after he had completed these literary labors did Wagner start writing the music which he composed in the proper sequence of the dramas, starting with *Das Rheingold,* then *Die Walküre,* then *Siegfried,* and finally *Götterdämmerung.*

The plot of *Die Walküre* centers around Siegmund and Sieglinde, two children whom the god Wotan had begotten upon earth. Having grown up in ignorance of each other, Siegmund and Sieglinde, the latter married to the gloomy warrior Hunding, fall in love when they first meet. Their action scandalizes the goddess Fricka, who is the spouse of Wotan, and so the latter sends the beautiful Valkyrie, Brunhilde, to punish the lovers. This warrior-maiden, however, disobeys Wotan by shielding the lovers. When she flees toward Walhalla, she is overtaken by the god and sentenced to slumber on a mountain top until rescued by some noble hero who would claim her as his bride.

GUIDE TO LISTENING

This excerpt, which is from the end of act three of the opera, deals with the scene in which the god Wotan, after bringing a magic sleep to the warrior-maiden Brunhilde, surrounds the mountain top where she lies with a wall of flames so that only a fearless knight could ascend to her and bring her back to life.

FOREST MURMURS
From "Siegfried"

FIRST PERFORMANCE OF THE OPERA: BAYREUTH, AUGUST 16, 1876

The stupendous task of writing the music for *Der Ring des Nibelungen*, the cycle of four dramas of which *Siegfried* is the third, occupied Wagner, with interruptions, about twenty years (1853–74).

In 1863, despairing of ever seeing the "Ring" produced, Wagner issued the entire poem in pamphlet form. In an introduction he expressed the hope that Destiny would direct to him some Prince, enlightened and powerful enough, to sponser the project which, as he now realized, would require the construction of a special theater.

A year later, the nineteen-year-old King of Bavaria, Ludwig II, saw the pamphlet and immediately sent for Wagner. He gave the composer a pension, established him in a handsome residence, and helped him to plan and erect a theater—the famous Festspielhaus in the little town of Bayreuth—in which the "Ring" could be properly presented. The composition of the music for *Siegfried*, which Wagner had been compelled to interrupt in 1857 ("When shall we meet again?" he wrote into the score in a note dated June 27, 1857) was now resumed. It was completed in 1871.

The plot of this opera, continuing the thread of the story told in *Die Walküre*, deals with Siegfried, the hero-son of Siegmund and Sieglinde. Brought up away from other beings by an ugly dwarf, Siegfried, upon reaching manhood, fashions himself a sword. With this weapon he slays the giant Fafner who has disguised himself as a dragon. After accidentally tasting the dragon's blood, Siegfried is magically rendered able to understand the chatter of the birds. From them he learns of the beautiful Brunhilde who sleeps on a mountain top surrounded by fire. Siegfried at once sets out to awaken the Valkyrie, and succeeds in penetrating the wall of fire that surrounds the mountain.

GUIDE TO LISTENING

The excerpt *Forest Murmurs* is from the second act of the music drama. Siegfried lies on the grass contemplating all of the familiar sounds of nature. He has just slain the dragon, Fafner, but does not know what this deed portends. When accidentally his finger, still moist with the dragon's blood, touches his lips, Siegfried becomes suddenly aware that he can understand the language of the birds.

GOOD FRIDAY SPELL
From "Parsifal"
FIRST PERFORMANCE OF THE MUSIC DRAMA: BAY-
REUTH, JUNE 26, 1882

The story of the legendary Knight, Parsi-fal, who gave up passion for eternal life, had gripped Wagner's imagination long before he was able to compose the music drama which bears that name. In 1857 he even planned to introduce Parsifal into the third act of *Tristan and Isolde* which he was then com-posing. This idea he abandoned. A little later, the beautiful spring weather on Good Friday in Switzerland where he was living, again brought Parsifal vividly before his mind. It was then that he sketched the Good Friday music, regarded by many as Wagner at his very best.

The plot of this music drama concerns the Holy Spear which pierced the side of our Savior, and which later was taken to a Temple Sanctuary in northern Spain, only to be stolen by the magician Klingsor. It also concerns Parsifal, a youth, guileless because he has spent his childhood in the desert. Parsifal undertakes to redeem the Holy Spear. After venturing to Klingsor's enchanted castle and withstanding the wiles of Kundry, the witch maiden, Parsifal possesses himself of the Holy Spear and brings it back to the Temple.

GUIDE TO LISTENING

The *Good Friday Spell* occurs in the latter part of act three of the music drama. Parsifal has returned with the Holy Spear to the Temple where he is hailed for his deed as the sovereign of the Knights of the Grail. He gazes at the meadow, the edge of the forest. "How fair this meadow is today," he says. "That is Good Friday's spell, my lord," he is told. All of nature glows with thankfulness on this day of love and sacrifice.

Carl Maria von Weber

BORN 1786 AT EUTIN, Germany, the son of an impressario who was a gentleman of fortune. Was taught the rudiments of music early, for his father, perhaps because he was Mozart's uncle by marriage, wanted to make virtuosi of all his sons and drilled them relentlessly. Carl Maria, the ninth child, responded to these disciplinarian methods by developing rapidly. At twelve he became a choirister, and it was then that his first compositions were published. At nineteen he had already composed four operas and had become a conductor. The year following he started working on *Der Freischutz* which was to make him famous as the founder of German national opera. The work was immediately successful, but von Weber's career was cut short, for he died in 1826 (aged 39) of consumption in London.

Carl Maria von Weber's music can be merely pleasantly tuneful. It can also be stirring, replete with melody which radiates a peculiarly penetrating brilliance, restless in mood and powerful in its impact.

For other works by the composer see *Recommended Recordings*.

"INVITATION TO A DANCE"

FIRST PERFORMANCE (AS ORCHESTRATED BY BERLIOZ): PARIS, WINTER, 1841

Weber, who was very much in love with his wife, composed this picturesque music for her. The year was 1819. Two decades later, Berlioz orchestrated the "Dance" so that it could be used in a Paris revival of von Weber's opera *Der Freischutz*. Years later, the conductor Felix Weingartner made a second orchestral version of this popular piece, originally composed for the piano.

GUIDE TO LISTENING

The work depicts exactly what its title suggests: a dancer inviting a lady to a dance; her evasive reply and eventual consent; their dance together; and, finally, his thanks and withdrawal.

Carl Maria von Weber

OVERTURE TO "DER FREISCHUTZ"

FIRST PERFORMANCE: OVERTURE: COPENHAGEN, OCTOBER 8, 1820; OPERA: BERLIN, JUNE 8, 1821

Although von Weber wrote a great deal of music of every kind, the best of his creative drive was directed into the composition of operas. Finding the field dominated by the Italians, he determined to put them to rout by writing an operatic work of definitely German coloring and feeling. This he accomplished in *Der Freischutz*, thereby initiating a new era in the history of the opera and paving the way for the appearance of Wagner.

The Overture was performed for the first time eight months ahead of the opera. It was played in Copenhagen where, from the Danish Queen, in place of pecuniary recompense von Weber received a golden snuff-box. Honored but not overjoyed, he said in a letter to his wife: "It is a very fine affair, but what am I supposed to do with all that sort of thing?"

GUIDE TO LISTENING

Most of the music of this stirring Overture is drawn from the body of the opera which deals with the vicissitudes of Max, a hunts-

[241]

man, who has recourse to the Demon, Zamiel, to win a contest for the place of Head Ranger. From the Demon he obtains seven magic bullets, and with these makes a perfect score. The final shot goes amiss, killing the dissolute Gaspar, who had led him astray. This forces Max to confess where he obtained the bullets, and he escapes punishment only through the pleas of Agatha, his fiancée.

OVERTURE TO "OBERON"

FIRST PERFORMANCE OF THE OPERA: LONDON, APRIL 12, 1826

Toward the end of his life von Weber was obsessed with the single thought (he knew that he was dying of consumption) of how best to provide for the future of his wife. In 1824 when he was offered a commission to write an opera for production at Covent Gardens in London, he accepted gladly, though his doctors had warned him that he could not live through the exertion of such a task. Disregarding their advice, von Weber went ahead. He even applied himself diligently to the study of English, for the libretto of *Oberon* was written in that language.

For this opera, which he completed on April 9, 1826, von Weber received five hun-

dred pound sterling; and, though he was
barely able to stand up without assistance, he
traveled to England to rehearse the work.
Two months after the opera's initial performance, he died quietly in England.

GUIDE TO LISTENING

The Overture faithfully reflects the different moods of the drama based on a very
old French romance. The impossibly complicated story deals with the king of the elves,
Oberon, and Titiana, who have vowed not to
be reconciled until they find a couple whose
love is stronger than temptation. Most of the
action takes place in Bagdad and Tunis as
well as in a rocky cavern on a desert island
where the fidelity of the lovers, Resia and
Huon, is put to the test.

◇◇◇◇◇◇◇◇◇◇◇◇◇◇◇◇◇◇◇◇◇◇◇◇◇◇

Recommended Recordings

Compiled by

GEORGE C. LESLIE
THE GRAMOPHONE SHOP
18 EAST 48TH STREET, NEW YORK

NOTE: Compositions marked with an asterisk (*) are those discussed in the book.

Abbreviations used in the following pages refer to record manufacturing companies, as follows:

C	-	Columbia (CM, Masterworks Set)
D	-	Decca
G	-	Gramophone (H.M.V.)
GT	-	Gamut
MC	-	Musicraft
TC	-	Technichord
V	-	Victor (VM, Masterpiece Set)

BACH, JOHANN SEBASTIAN

* *Brandenburg Concertos (6)*
Busch Chamber Players, conducted by Adolf
Busch. Fourteen 12″ discs, in Set CM–
249/50.
OTHER WORKS BY J. S. BACH:
Nine Chorale-Preludes
(Including the six Schübler Chorale-Prel-
udes).
Carl Weinrich (Westminster Choir School
Organ).
Five 10″ discs, in Set MC–22.
Concerto in D Minor
Edwin Fischer and Orchestra. Three 12″
discs, in Set VM–252.
*Suite No. 1, in C Major & Suite No. 2, in B
Minor*
The Adolf Busch Chamber Players, con-
ducted by Adolf Busch. Six 12″ discs, in
Set VM–332.
Toccatas and Fugues
Toccata and Fugue in D Minor; Toccata
and Fugue in F Major; Fugue in F Major;
Toccata (with two fugues) in E Major.
Carl Weinrich ("Praetorious" Organ of
Westminster Choir School, Princeton, N. J.).
Four 12″ discs, in Set MC–36.
Organ Recital of the Music of Bach
Containing: "Vivaldi" Concerto No. 2, in

A Minor; Chorale-Prelude—"Wachet auf!":
Prelude and Fugue in E flat Major (St.
Anna Fugue); Trio-Sonata No. 1, in E
flat Major. E. Power Biggs (Organ of
the Germanic Museum, Cambridge, Mass).
Five 12″ discs, in Set TC–1.

BACH, JOHANN CHRISTIAN

Harpsichord Concerto in G Major
Marguerite Roesgen-Champion (Harpsi-
chord) and String Trio. Two 10″ discs,
Nos. V–4441/42.

BACH, CARL PHILLIP EMANUEL

Concerto for orchestra in D Major
  (arr. M. Steinberg)
Boston Symphony Orchestra, conducted by
Serge Koussevitzky. Two 12″ discs, in Set
VM–559.

BEETHOVEN, LUDWIG VAN

* *Symphony No. 3 in E-flat Major, Op. 55,*
("Eroica")
Vienna Philharmonic Orchestra, conducted
by Felix Weingartner. Six 12″ discs, in Set
CM–285.
* *Overture to "Leonore" No. 3, Op. 72*
Vienna Philharmonic Orchestra, conducted
by Bruno Walter. Two 12″ discs, in Set
VM–359.

Recommended Recordings

* Concerto (Violin and Orchestra) in D Major, Op. 61

Josef Szigeti and Symphony Orchestra, conducted by Bruno Walter. Five 12″ discs, in Set CM–177.

* Overture to "Coriolanus" Op. 62

London Symphony Orchestra, conducted by Bruno Walter. 12″ disc, No. v–12535.

However, though not as recent a recording the following reading is the finest from an interpretative view.

B. B. C. Symphony Orchestra, conducted by Sir Adrian Boult. 12″ disc, No. v–11909.

* Symphony No. 5 in C Minor, Op. 67

London Philharmonic Orchestra, conducted by Felix Weingartner. Four 12″ discs, in Set CM–254.

Also recommended is the less orthodox reading:

Berlin Philharmonic Orchestra, conducted by Wilhelm Furtwängler. Five 12″ discs, in Set VM–426.

* Symphony No. 6 in F Major, Op. 68 ("Pastoral")

B. B. C. Symphony Orchestra, conducted by Arturo Toscanini. Five 12″ discs, in Set VM–417.

* Concerto (Piano and Orchestra) No. 5 in E-flat Major, Op. 73 ("Emperor")

Artur Schnabel and London Philharmonic
Orchestra, conducted by Malcolm Sargent
Five 12″ discs, in Set VM–155.

* *Overture to Goethe's "Egmont," Op. 84*
Vienna Philharmonic Orchestra, conducted
by Felix Weingartner. 12″ disc, No. C–
69195D.

* *Symphony No. 7 in A Major, Op. 92*
Vienna Philharmonic Orchestra, conducted
by Felix Weingartner. Five 12″ discs, in
Set CM–260.
This orthodox reading is preferred to the
exciting but individual treatment by Toscanini, listed below:
New York Philharmonic-Symphony Orchestra, conducted by Arturo Toscanini. Five
12″ discs, in Set VM–317.

* *Symphony No. 9 in D Minor, Op. 125,*
("Choral")
Until Weingartner rerecords this symphony
the present version is the best.
Soloists, Chorus and Vienna Philharmonic
Orchestra, conducted by Felix Weingartner.
Eight 12″ discs, in Set CM–227.

OTHER WORKS BY BEETHOVEN:

Sonata (Piano) No. 8, in C Minor, Op. 13
("Pathetique")

Recommended Recordings

Wilhelm Kempff. Two 12″ imported discs, Nos. D–X202/3.

Sonata (Piano) in C sharp Minor, Op. 27, No. 2 ("Moonlight")

Ignace Jan Paderewski. Two 12″ discs, in Set VM–349. (Also—Paderewski: Minuet in G, Op. 14, No. 1).

Sonata (Piano) in B flat Major, Op. 106 ("Hammerklavier")

Wilhelm Kempff. Six 12″ imported discs, Nos. D–CA8254/58.

String Quartet No. 8, in E Minor, Op. 59, No. 2

Budapest String Quartet. Four 12″ discs, in Set VM–340.

String Quartet No. 14, in C sharp Minor, Op. 131

Budapest String Quartet. Five 12″ discs, in Set CM–429.

Septet in E flat Major (for violin, viola, 'cello, string bass, clarinet, bassoon and horn), Op. 20

A. Catterall, B. Schore, A. Gauntlett, E. Cruft, F. Thurston, A. Camden, A. Thonger. Five 12″ discs, in Set VM–571.

Overture—Die Weihe des Hauses, Op. 124 ("Consecration of the House")

London Philharmonic Orchestra, conducted by Felix Weingartner. Two 12″ discs, in

Set CM–X140. (Also—Egmont, Op. 84—
Clärchens Tod).

Symphony No. 4, in B flat Major, Op. 60
B. B. C. Symphony Orchestra, conducted by
Arturo Toscanini. Four 12″ discs, in Set
VM–676.

Ah, perfido! Op. 65
Kirsten Flagstad and the Philadelphia Orchestra, conducted by Eugene Ormandy.
One 12″ and one 10″ disc, in Set VM–
439.

BERLIOZ, HECTOR

* *Symphonie Fantastique, Op. 14–A*
Paris Symphony Orchestra, conducted by
Pierre Monteux. Six 12″ discs, in Set VM–
111.
Or: Newer recording but not as good an
interpretation:
Paris Conservatory Orchestra, conducted by
Bruno Walter. Six 12″ discs, in Set VM–
662.

* *Excerpts from "The Damnation of Faust,"
Op. 24*
March hongroise; Danse des Sylphes (Act
I); Menuet des Feux-Follets and Presto,
(Act III). London Philharmonic Orches-
tra, conducted by Sir Thomas Beecham
Two 12″ discs, in Set CM–X94.

Recommended Recordings

BIZET, GEORGES

* *Suite No. 1 from "L'Arlésienne"*
Philadelphia Orchestra, conducted by Leopold Stokowski. Three 12″ discs, in Set VM–62.

Carmen—Opera in 4 acts
Complete Recording. Paris Opéra-Comique. Fifteen 12″ discs, in Set CM–01.
Carmen Suite. London Philharmonic Orchestra, conducted by Sir Thomas Beecham. Two 12″ discs, in Set CM–X144.

BORODIN, ALEXANDER

* *Symphony No. 2 in B Minor*
London Symphony Orchestra, conducted by Albert Coates. Three 12″ discs, in Set VM–113.

In the Steppes of Central Asia—Symphonic Poem
London Symphony Orchestra, conducted by Albert Coates. 12″ disc, No. V–11169.

String Quartet No. 2, in D Major
Pro Arte Quartet. Four 12″ discs, in Set VM–255.

Prince Igor—Opera in 4 acts
Arioso of Jaroslavna, (Act I) & (Rimsky-Korsakov: Sadko-Berceuse). Nina Koshetz

(soprano, in Russian) with Orchestra. 12″
disc, No. v–9233.

Vladimir's Cavatina. See: Tchaikowsky:
Eugene Onegin.

No sleep, no rest, (Act II). Georges Bak-
lanoff (baritone, in Russian) with Orchestra. 12″ disc, No. D–25122.

Polovetsian Dances. Leeds Festival Choir,
London Philharmonic Orchestra, conducted
by Sir Thomas Beecham. Two 12″ discs, in
Set CM–X54.

BRAHMS, JOHANNES

* *Symphony No. 1 in C Minor, Op. 68*
London Symphony Orchestra, conducted by
Felix Weingartner. Five 12″ discs, in Set
CM–383.

* *Symphony No. 2 in D Major, Op. 73*
London Philharmonic Orchestra, conducted
by John Barbirolli. Five 12″ discs, in Set
CM–412.

* *Concerto (Violin and Orchestra) in D Major,*
Op. 77
Joseph Szigeti and the Halle Orchestra, conducted by Sir Hamilton Harty. Five 12″
discs, in Set CM–117.

The finest interpretation. Also recommended:

Recommended Recordings

Jascha Heifetz and Boston Symphony Orchestra, conducted by Serge Koussevitzky. Five 12″ discs, in Set VM-581.

* *Academic Festival Overture, Op. 80*
Vienna Philharmonic Orchestra, conducted by Bruno Walter. 12″ disc, No. V-12190.

* *Tragic Overture, Op. 81*
London Philharmonic Orchestra, conducted by Sir Thomas Beecham. Two 12″ discs, in Set CM-X85.

* *Concerto (Piano and Orchestra) No. 2 in B-flat Major, Op. 83*
Vladimir Horowitz and the N. B. C. Symphony Orchestra, conducted by Arturo Toscanini. Six 12″ discs, in Set VM-740.

* *Symphony No. 3 in F Major, Op. 90*
London Philharmonic Orchestra, conducted by Felix Weingartner. Four 12″ discs, in Set CM-353.

* *Symphony No. 4 in E Minor, Op. 98*
London Symphony Orchestra, conducted by Felix Weingartner. Five 12″ discs, in Set CM-335.

OTHER WORKS BY BRAHMS:

Piano Quintet, Op. 34
Rudolf Serkin and Busch Quartet. Five 12″ discs, in Set VM-607.
Trio for violin, piano, and horn, Op. 40

Recommended Recordings

Adolf Busch, Aubrey Brain, and Rudolf
Serkin. Four 12″ discs, in Set VM–199.

String Quartet, Op. 51

Busch Quartet. Four 12″ discs, in Set VM–227.

Variations on a theme by Haydn, Op. 56

London Philharmonic Orchestra, conducted
by Felix Weingartner. Two 12″ discs, in
Set CM–X125.

Also recommended: New York Philharmonic-Symphony, conducted by Arturo Toscanini. Two 12″ discs, in Set VM–355.

Double Concerto for violin, 'cello and orchestra, Op. 102

Jacques Thibaud, Pablo Casals with Casals
Orchestra, conducted by Alfred Cortot.
Four 12″ discs, in Set VM–99.

Clarinet Quintet in B Minor, Op. 115

Reginald Kell and Busch Quartet. Four
12″ discs, in Set VM–491.

Lieder

Song Society. Alexander Kipnis (bass, in
German) with Gerald Moore (piano). Six
12″ discs, in Set VM–522.

Containing: Four Serious Songs; Von weiger
liebe; Die Mainacht; etc.

Elena Gerhardt New Selection of Songs
(1939). Elena Gerhardt (mezzo-soprano,

in German) with Gerald Moore (piano).
Six 10″ imported discs, in album. (Gramophone Shop, N. Y.)
Containing: Zigeunerlieder; Der Tod das ist
die Kühle Nacht; Der Gang zum Liebchen;
Therese, and songs by Schubert and Hugo
Wolf. This album is especially recommended as one of the finest examples of
Lieder singing to be found on discs.
Immer leiser wird mein Schlummer, Op.
105, No. 2. Elizabeth Schumann (soprano,
in German) with piano & Mendelssohn:
Auf flügeln des gesanges). 10″ disc, No.
v–1837.

CARPENTER, JOHN ALDEN

* *Adventures in a Perambulator*—Suite for
orchestra
  Minneapolis Symphony Orchestra, conducted by Eugene Ormandy. Four 12″
  discs, in Set vm–238.
Skyscrapers—jazz ballet
  Victor Symphony Orchestra, conducted by
  Nat. Shilkret. Three 12″ discs, in Set vm–
  130.

CHOPIN, FRÉDÉRIC

* *Concerto (Piano and Orchestra) No. 1 in E
Minor, Op. 11*
  Arthur Rubinstein and London Symphony

Orchestra, conducted by John Barbirolli.
Four 12″ discs, in Set VM–418.

* *Concerto (Piano and Orchestra) No. 2 in F Minor, Op. 21*
Alfred Cortot and Orchestra, conducted by John Barbirolli. Four 12″ discs, in Set VM–567.

Sonata No. 3, in B Minor, Op. 58
Alexander Brailowsky (piano). Three 12″ discs, in Set VM–548.

Piano Music of Chopin
Containing: Chant Polonaise No. 1 (trans. Liszt); Mazurkas in A flat Major, Op. 50, No. 2; B Minor, Op. 33, No. 4; Nocturne in E flat Major, Op. 9, No. 2; Nocturne in D flat Major, Op. 27, No. 2; Preludes—Nos. 6, 3, and 7; Waltz in A flat Major, Op. 42; Waltz in C sharp Minor, Op. 64, No. 2. Moriz Rosenthal (piano). Four 12″ discs, in Set VM–338.

DEBUSSY, CLAUDE

* *"Prelude to the Afternoon of a Faun"*
London Symphony Orchestra, conducted by Sir Thomas Beecham. 12″ disc, No. C–69600D.

* *Nocturnes: Clouds; Festivals; Sirens*
Philadelphia Orchestra, conducted by Leopold Stokowski. Three 12″ and one 10″ discs, in Set VM–630.

Recommended Recordings

* *La Mer*—Three Symphonic Sketches
Boston Symphony Orchestra, conducted by Serge Koussevitzky. Three 12″ discs, in Set VM-643.

OTHER WORKS BY DEBUSSY:

String Quartet in G Minor, Op. 10
Pro Arte String Quartet. Four 12″ discs, in Set VM-186.

Iberia—Suite for Orchestra
New York Philharmonic-Symphony, conducted by John Barbirolli. Three 12″ discs, in Set VM-460.
(This recording is listed as it is the best technically, although no recording has as yet fully realized the composer's intentions.)

Pelléas and Mélisande—Opera in 5 acts
Selected Passages: Soloists of the Paris Opéra and Opéra Comique with Symphony Orchestra, conducted by Piero Coppola. Set VM-68.

Piano Music of Debussy
Contains: Children's Corner Suite; Suite Bergamasque; Soirée dans Granade; Réflets dans l'Eau; Cathédrale Engloutie. Walter Gieseking. Two 10″ and four 12″ discs, in Set CM-314.

Songs (14) of Debussy
Contains: Fêtes Galantes; Trois Chansons

de Bilitis; Le Promenoir des deux Amants;
Ballade des femmes de Paris; De Grève.
Maggie Teyte (soprano, in French) with
Alfred Cortot (piano). Seven 10″ discs, in
Set VM–322.

DUKAS, PAUL

* *The Sorcerer's Apprentice*—Scherzo for or-
chestra
Paris Conservatory Orchestra, conducted by
Philippe Gaubert. Two 12″ discs, in Set
CM–X75.
The Toscanini version, while exciting, is
not in the Gallic frame.
New York Philharmonic-Symphony, con-
ducted by Arturo Toscanini. 12″ disc, No.
V–7021.

DVOŘÁK, ANTONIN

* *Symphony No. 5 in E Minor, Op 95 ("From
the New World")*
Czech Philharmonic Orchestra, conducted
by Georg Szell. Five 12″ discs, in Set VM–
469.

OTHER WORKS BY DVOŘÁK:

Slavonic Dances
16 Slavonic Dances in Sets VM–310 and VM–
345. Czech Philharmonic Orchestra, conducted by Vaclav Talich.

Recommended Recordings

String Quartet in E flat Major, Op. 51
Léner String Quartet. Four 12″ discs, in Set CM–369.

Symphony No. 2, in D Minor, Op. 70
Czech Philharmonic Orchestra, conducted by Vaclav Talich. Five 12″ discs, in Set VM–663.

Piano Quintet in A Major, Op. 81
Artur Schnabel and Pro Arte Quartet. Four 12″ discs, in Set VM–219.

String Quartet in F Major, Op. 96
Budapest String Quartet. Three 12″ discs, in Set VM–681.

ENESCO, GEORGES

* *Roumanian Rhapsody No. 1 in A Major, Op. 11*
Minneapolis Symphony Orchestra, conducted by Eugene Ormandy. Two 10″ discs, Nos. V–1701/2.

FRANCK, CÉSAR

* *Symphonic Variations* (1885)
Walter Gieseking and London Philharmonic Orchestra, conducted by Sir Henry Wood. Two 12″ discs in Set CM–X10.
Also recommended:
Alfred Cortot and London Philharmonic Orchestra, conducted by Landon Ronald. Two 12″ discs, Nos. V–8357/58. Though

an older recording, the Cortot-Ronald version is preferred by many.

* *Symphony in D Minor* (1886–88)
Lamoureux Orchestra, conducted by Albert Wolff. Four 12″ imported discs, Nos. D–CA128/31.

OTHER WORKS BY FRANCK:

Prelude, Chorale and Fugue (1884)
Egon Petri (piano). Two 12″ discs, in Set CM–X176.

Sonata for violin and piano (1886)
Alfred Dubois and Marcel Mass. Four 12″ discs, in Set CM–158.

String Quartet in D Major (1889)
Pro Arte Quartet. Five 12″ discs, in Set VM–259.

Three Chorals for Organ (1890)
Chorale No. 1, in E Major (only).
Albert Schweitzer (Ste. Aurelie, Strasbourg). Two 12″ discs, in Set CM–X100.

GERSHWIN, GEORGE

* *Concerto in F Major (Piano and Orchestra)*
Jesús María Sanromá and the Boston "Pops" Orchestra, conducted by Arthur Fiedler. Four 12″ discs, in Set VM–690.

(Only authentic recording in which the

complete symphonic score as the composer
wrote it is utilized.)

Rhapsody in Blue
Jesús María Sanromá and the Boston "Pops"
Orchestra, conducted by Arthur Fiedler.
Two 12″ discs, in Set VM–358.

An American in Paris—Symphonic Poem
Victor Symphony Orchestra, conducted by
N. Shilkret. Two 12″ discs, Nos. V–
35963/64.

Porgy and Bess—Selections
Anne Brown (soprano), Todd Duncan
(baritone), with the Eva Jessye Choir and
the Decca Symphony Orchestra, conducted
by Alexander Smallens. Four 12″ discs, in
Set D–145.

GLINKA, MICHAEL

* *Overture to "Russlan and Ludmilla"*
Boston "Pops" Orchestra, conducted by
Arthur Fiedler. 10″ disc, No. V–4427.

Kamarinskaya—Orchestral Fantasia
London Symphony Orchestra, conducted by
Albert Coates. 12″ disc, No. V–11482.

GRIEG, EDVARD

* *Concerto (Piano and Orchestra) in A Minor,*
Op. 16
Wilhelm Bachaus and Symphony Orches-

tra, conducted by John Barbirolli. Three
12″ discs, in Set VM–204.

Peer Gynt Suite No. 1
London Philharmonic, conducted by Sir
Thomas Beecham. Two 12″ discs, in Set
CM–X180.

Peer Gynt Suite No. 2
New Light Symphony Orchestra, conducted
by Eugene Goossens. Two 12″ discs, Nos.
V–9327/28.

GRIFFES, CHARLES T.

* *The White Peacock*
Columbia Broadcasting Symphony, con-
ducted by Howard Barlow. 10″ disc, No.
C–17140D.

The Pleasure Dome of Kubla Khan—Symphonic Poem
Minneapolis Symphony Orchestra, conducted by Eugene Ormandy. 12″ disc, No.
V–7957.

HANDEL, GEORGE F.

* *"Water Music"*
London Philharmonic Orchestra, conducted
by Sir Hamilton Harty. Two 12″ discs, in
Set CM–X13.

Royal Fireworks Music (Trans. Harty)
London Philharmonic Orchestra, conducted

by Sir Hamilton Harty. Two 12″ discs, in
Set CM–X51.

Concerto Grosso in D Major, Op. 6, No. 5
London Philharmonic Orchestra, conducted
by Felix Weingartner. Two 12″ discs, in
Set CM–X142.

Concerto Grosso in G Minor, Op. 6, No. 6
London Symphony Orchestra, conducted by
Felix Weingartner. Two 12″ discs, in Set
CM–X154.

HAYDN, JOSEPH

* *Symphony No. 94 in G Major ("Surprise")*
Boston Symphony Orchestra, conducted by
Serge Koussevitzky. Three 12″ discs, in Set
VM–55.
Or: Newer recording but not as good an
interpretation:
Columbia Broadcasting Symphony, con-
ducted by Howard Barlow. Three 12″ discs,
in Set CM–363.

* *Symphony No. 101, in D Major, ("The
Clock")*
New York Philharmonic-Symphony, conducted by Arturo Toscanini. Four 12″
discs, in Set VM–57.

* *Symphony No. 104 in D Major ("London")*
London Philharmonic Orchestra, conducted
by Sir Thomas Beecham. Three 12″ discs,
in Set CM–409.

Recommended Recordings

OTHER WORKS BY HAYDN:

Symphony No. 67 in F Major; Symphony No. 80 in D Minor
  (Edited by Alfred Einstein)
  Orchestra of the New Friends of Music, conducted by Fritz Stiedry. Five 12″ discs, in Set VM–536.

Symphony No. 100, in G Major ("Military")
  Vienna Philharmonic Orchestra, conducted by Bruno Walter. Three 12″ discs, in Set VM–472.

Volume VIII of the Haydn Quartet Society
  B flat Major, Op. 1, No. 1
  E flat Major, Op. 20, No. 1
  B flat Major, Op. 55, No. 3
  B flat Major, Op. 76, No. 4
  Pro Arte Quartet. Seven 12″ discs, in Set VM–595.

The Creation—oratorio
  Auf starken Fittige schwingt sich der Adlen stolz (Tauben arie). Eide Norena (Soprano, in German) with Orchestra. 12″ disc, No. V–15182 (& Handel: Atalanta—Care selve).

IPPOLITOV-IVANOV, MICHAIL

* *Caucasian Sketches*—Suite for Orchestra
  Berlin Philharmonic Orchestra, conducted by Alois Melichar. Three 10″ imported discs, Nos. D–P05069/70 & P05092.

Recommended Recordings

Excerpts:

In the Village. The Philadelphia Orchestra, conducted by Leopold Stokowski. 12″ disc, No. v-6514. (Also Borodin: Prince Igor-Polovetzki Dance).

March of the Caucasian Chief. The Philadelphia Orchestra, conducted by Leopold Stokowski, 10″ disc, No. v-1335 (Also Glazounov: Danse Oriental).

LISZT, FRANZ

* Les Préludes—Symphonic Poem
Paris Philharmonic Orchestra, conducted by Selmar Meyrowitz. Two 12″ discs, in Set cm-x82.

Orpheus—Symphonic Poem
The Columbia Broadcasting Symphony, conducted by Howard Barlow. Two 12″ discs, in Set cm-165.

Totentanz (Paraphrase on Dies Irae")
Edward Kilenyi and the Paris Symphony, conducted by Selmar Meyrowitz. Two 12″ discs, in Set cm-x122.

MacDOWELL, EDWARD

* Concerto (Piano and Orchestra) No. 2 in D Minor, Op. 23
Jesús María Sanromá with Boston "Pops"

Orchestra, conducted by Arthur Fiedler. In
Set VM–324.

Second (Indian) Suite for Orchestra

Columbia Broadcasting Symphony, conducted by Howard Barlow. Four 12″ discs,
in Set CM–373.

MENDELSSOHN, FELIX

* *Excerpts from "A Midsummer Night's
Dream"*

Overture & Wedding March. Boston "Pops"
Orchestra, conducted by Arthur Fiedler.
Two 12″ discs, Nos. V–11919/20.

Scherzo—included in Haydn: Symphony
No. 102—"The Clock."

Nocturne—B.B.C. Symphony Orchestra, conducted by Sir Adrian Boult. 10″ disc, No.
V–4312.

* *Symphony No. 4 in A Major, Op. 90 ("Italian")*

Boston Symphony Orchestra, conducted by
Serge Koussevitzky. Three 12″ discs, in Set
VM–294.

OTHER WORKS BY MENDELSSOHN:

Hebrides (Fingal's Cave) Overture

London Philharmonic Orchestra, conducted
by Sir Thomas Beecham. 12″ disc, No.
C–69400D.

Recommended Recordings

Symphony No. 3 in A Minor, Op. 56, ("Scotch")
    Royal Philharmonic Orchestra, conducted by Felix Weingartner. Four 12″ discs, in Set CM–126.

Concerto (Violin and Orchestra) in E Minor, Op. 64
    Yehudi Menuhin and Paris Conservatory Orchestra, conducted by Georges Enesco. Four 12″ discs, in Set VM–531.

Elijah—Oratorio
    If with all your hearts (No. 4) & Then shall the righteous shine (No. 39). Webster Booth (tenor, in English) with London Philharmonic Orchestra, conducted by W. Braithwaite. 12″ disc, No. V–12609.

MOUSSORGSKY, MODESTE

* *Pictures at an Exhibition*
    No good piano recording available.
    Orchestrated by Maurice Ravel:
    Boston Symphony Orchestra, conducted by Serge Koussevitzky. Four 12″ discs, in Set VM–102.

Boris Godounov—Music drama in 4 acts
    Orchestral Synthesis (arr. Stokowski from original score). Philadelphia Orchestra, conducted by Leopold Stokowski. Three 12″ discs, in Set VM–391.

[268]

Coronation Scene. Fedor Chaliapin with Chorus and Orchestra. 12″ disc, No. v-11485.

Monologue—I have attained the highest power (Act II). Fedor Chaliapin with Orchestra. 12″ v-14517. (Clock Scene—Ah! I am Suffocating).

Marina's Dressing Room—Maidens Chorus & Polonaise. Riga Opera Chorus. 12″ disc, No. D-25403.

Prayer and Death of Boris. Fedor Chaliapin with Orchestra. 12″ disc, No. v-15177.

Khovantchina—Music drama in 5 acts
Prelude: Boston Symphony Orchestra, conducted by Serge Koussevitzky. 12″ disc, No. v-14415.

Dance of the Persian Slaves. London Symphony Orchestra, conducted by Albert Coates. 12″ disc, No. v-11135.

Songs and Dances of Death—a song cycle
Moshe Rudinow (baritone, in Russian) with piano accompaniment. G.T. Set MS5.

Without Sunlight—a song cycle
In collection of Songs—Vol. I. Without Sunlight; Pride; Ballade, and King Saul. Moshe Rudinow (baritone, in Russian) with piano accompaniment. G.T. Set MS4.

Recommended Recordings

MOZART, WOLFGANG AMADEUS

* *Symphony No. 40 in G Minor, K–550*

London Philharmonic Orchestra, conducted by Sir Thomas Beecham. Three 12″ discs, in Set CM–316.

* *Symphony No. 41 in C Major K–551 ("Jupiter")*

London Philharmonic Orchestra, conducted by Sir Thomas Beecham. Four 12″ discs, in Set CM–194.

This reading is to be preferred to the one listed below, which is more recent but does not catch the spirit of the composition as fully.

Vienna Philharmonic Orchestra, conducted by Bruno Walter. Four 12″ discs, in Set VM–584.

OTHER WORKS BY MOZART:

Concerto No. 4 (Violin and Orchestra), in D Major, K. 218

Joseph Szigeti and the London Philharmonic Orchestra, conducted by Sir Thomas Beecham (Joachim cadenzas used). Three 12″ discs, in Set CM–224.

Or:

Fritz Kreisler and the London Philharmonic Orchestra, conducted by Malcolm Sargent. Three 12″ discs, in Set VM–623 (the Kreisler cadenzas are used).

Recommended Recordings

Concerto (Piano and Orchestra), No. 9 in E flat Major, K. 271

Walter Gieseking and the Berlin State Opera Orchestra, conducted by Hans Rosbaud. Four 12″ discs, in Set CM–291.

Symphony No. 35, in D Major, K. 385 ("Haffner")

London Philharmonic Orchestra, conducted by Sir Thomas Beecham. Three 12″ discs (5 sides, last side blank), in Set CM–399.

Concerto (Piano and Orchestra), No. 14 in E flat Major, K. 449

Rudolf Serkin and the Busch Chamber Players, conducted by Adolf Busch. Three 12″ discs, in Set VM–657.

Piano Quintet in G Minor, K–516

Pro Arte Quartet and A. Hobday. Four 12″ discs, in Set VM–190.

Serenade in G Major, K. 525 ("Eine kleine Nachtmusik")

Berlin Philharmonic Orchestra, conducted by Wilhelm Furtwängler. Three 12″ imported discs, Nos. D–X211/3.

Or:

Vienna Philharmonic Orchestra, conducted by Bruno Walter. Two 12″ discs, in Set VM–364.

Symphony No. 39 in E-flat Major, K–543

B.B.C. Symphony Orchestra, conducted by

Bruno Walter. Three 12″ discs, in Set
VM–258.

Clarinet Quintet in A Major, K–581
Benny Goodman and the Budapest String
Quartet. Three 10″ and one 12″ discs, in
Set VM–452.

Le Nozzie di Figaro—Complete Recording
The Glyndebourne Festival Opera Company, conducted by Fritz Busch. Seventeen
12″ discs, in Sets VM–313/315.

Die Zauberflöte—Complete Recording
Mozart Opera Society Recording, Famous
Artists, Berlin Philharmonic Orchestra,
conducted by Sir Thomas Beecham. Nineteen 12″ discs, in Sets VM–541/542.

PROKOFIEFF, SERGE

* *Classical Symphony in D Major, Op. 25*
Boston Symphony Orchestra, conducted by
Serge Koussevitzky. Two 12″ discs, Nos.
V–7196/97. (Includes: Love for Three
Oranges—March and Scherzo).

OTHER WORKS BY PROKOFIEFF:

*Concerto (Violin and Orchestra) No. 1 in D
Major, Op. 19*
Joseph Szigeti and London Philharmonic
Orchestra, conducted by Sir Thomas

Beecham. Three 12″ discs, in Set CM–244.

Concerto (Piano and Orchestra) No. 3 in C Major, Op. 26

Serge Prokofieff and London Symphony Orchestra, conducted by Piero Coppola. Three 12″ discs, in Set VM–176.

Lieutenant Kijé—Symphonic Suite, Op. 60

Boston Symphony Orchestra, conducted by Serge Koussevitzky. Three 12″ discs, in Set VM–459 (also includes March and Scherzo from The Love for Three Oranges) .

Concerto (Violin and Orchestra) No. 2 in G Minor, Op. 63

Jascha Heifetz and Boston Symphony Orchestra, conducted by Serge Koussevitzky. Three 12″ discs, in Set VM–450.

Peter and the Wolf—Symphonic Fairy Tale for Children, Op. 67

Boston Symphony Orchestra, conducted by Serge Koussevitzky and narrated by Richard Hale. Three 12″ discs, in Set VM–566.

The Love of Three Oranges—Opera in 4 acts Symphonic Suite.

Orchestra des Concerts Poulet, conducted by Gaston Poulet. Three 12″ discs, Nos. D–25123/25.

See: Lieutenant Kijé and Classical Symphony for other recordings of March and Scherzo.

Recommended Recordings

RACHMANINOFF, SERGEI

* *Piano Concerto No. 2 in C Minor, Op. 18*
  Sergei Rachmaninoff with Philadelphia Orchestra, conducted by Leopold Stokowski. Five 12″ discs, in Set VM–58.
  Authentic recording by the composer stands up well against the more recent version listed below:
  Benno Moiseivitsch and the London Philharmonic conducted by Walter Goehr. Four 12″ discs, in Set VM–666.
* *Symphony No. 2 in E Minor, Op. 27*
  Minneapolis Symphony Orchestra, conducted by Eugene Ormandy. Six 12″ discs, in Set VM–239.

OTHER WORKS BY RACHMANINOFF:

The Isle of the Dead—Tone Poem, Op. 29
  Philadelphia Orchestra, conducted by Sergei Rachmaninoff. With Vocalise, Op. 34, No. 14. Three 12″ discs, in Set VM–75.
Piano Concerto No. 3, D Minor, Op. 30
  Sergei Rachmaninoff with Philadelphia Orchestra, conducted by Eugene Ormandy. Op. 23. Five 12″ discs, in Set VM–710.
Eleven Piano Pieces by Sergei Rachmaninoff (composer at the piano). Five 10″ discs, in Set VM–722.

Recommended Recordings

Rhapsody on a Theme of Paganini, Op. 43
  Sergei Rachmaninoff with Philadelphia Orchestra, conducted by Leopold Stokowski. Three 12″ discs, in Set VM-250.

Symphony No. 3, in A Minor, Op. 44
  Philadelphia Orchestra conducted by Sergei Rachmaninoff. Five 12″ discs (9 sides, last side blank) in Set VM-712.

RAVEL, MAURICE

* *Daphnis and Chloé*—Second Orchestral Suite (1909–11)
  Philadelphia Orchestra, conducted by Eugene Ormandy. Two 12″ discs, in Set VM-667.
  This brilliant recording in no way diminishes Dr. Koussevitzky's remarkably sensitive interpretation.
  Boston Symphony Orchestra, conducted by Serge Koussevitzky. Two 12″ discs, Nos. V-7143/44.

* *Boléro* (1928)
  Lamoureux Orchestra, conducted by Maurice Ravel. Two 12″ discs, Nos. D-CA8015/16. (Note: This is the correct Ballet version.

Recommended Recordings

OTHER WORKS BY RAVEL:

Pavanne pour une Infante défunte (1899)
Arranged for Orchestra by the composer.
Symphony Orchestra, conducted by Piero
Coppola. 12″ disc, No. v–9306.
(Also contains: L'Enfant et Les Sortileges
—Five O'clock) .

String Quartet in F (1902–03)
The Budapest String Quartet. Four 12″
discs, in Set CM–425.

Alborada del Gracioso (1905)
Walter Gieseking (piano). 10″ disc, No.
C–17137D.

Introduction and Allegro for Harp with ac-
companiment by String Quartet, Flute and
Clarinet (1906)
Laura Newell (Harp), Stuyvesant String
Quartet, John Wummer and Ralph Mc-
Lane. Two 12″ discs, in Set CM–X167.

Gaspard de la Nuit (1908)
Complete, including: Ondine, Scarbo, and
Le Gibet. Walter Gieseking (piano).
Two 12″ discs, in Set CM–X141.

Mother Goose Suite (1908; orch. 1912)
Columbia Broadcasting Symphony, conducted by Howard Barlow. Two 12″ discs,
in Set CM–X151.

Or:

Boston Symphony Orchestra, conducted by
Serge Koussevitzky. Two 12" discs, Nos.
v–7370/71.

Le Tombeau de Couperin (1914–17)
Paris Conservatory Orchestra, conducted by
Piero Coppola. Two 12" discs, Nos. v–
12320/21.

La Valse (1920)
Boston Symphony Orchestra, conducted by
Serge Koussevitzky. Two 12" discs, Nos.
v–7413/14.

RIMSKY-KORSAKOFF, NICHOLAS

* *Scheherazade*—Symphonic Suite
The Cleveland Orchestra, conducted by
Artur Rodzinski. Five 12" discs, in Set
cm–398.
Or version used for Ballets Russes:
London Philharmonic Orchestra, conducted
by Antal Dorati. Five 12" discs, in Set
vm–509.

* *The Golden Cockerel*—Symphonic Suite
London Symphony Orchestra, conducted by
Eugene Goossens. Three 12" discs, in Set
vm–504.

Sadko—Opera in 4 acts
Song of the Indian Guest (Chanson Hin-
doue) B. Gigli with Orchestra. v–1570.

Recommended Recordings

Berceuse (Scene 7). See: A. Borodin: Prince Igor.

Song of the Viking Guest, Scene 4, Fedor Chaliapin with Orchestra. 12″ disc, No. v-6867. (Also includes Borodin: Prince Igor—How goes it Prince?)

ROSSINI, GIOACCHINO

* *Overture to "The Barber of Seville"*
Berlin Philharmonic Orchestra, conducted by Wilhelm Furtwängler. 12″ disc, imported, No. D-CA8218.

Or:

New York Philharmonic-Symphony, conducted by Arturo Toscanini. 12″ disc, No. v-7255.

An interesting comparison of two renowned conductors' treatment of this popular Overture.

Overture to "Scala di Seta"
London Philharmonic Orchestra, conducted by Sir Thomas Beecham. 12″ disc, No. c-9077M.

Or:

B.B.C. Symphony Orchestra, conducted by Arturo Toscanini. 12″ disc, No. v-15191. The popular British conductor gives a more satisfying performance.

Recommended Recordings

Overture to "Semiramide"
New York Philharmonic-Symphony, conducted by Arturo Toscanini. Two 12" discs, in Set VM–408.

Overture to "William Tell"
London Philharmonic Orchestra, conducted by Sir Thomas Beecham. Two 12" discs, in Set CM–x60.
The following reading by Toscanini is marred by the sudden breaks. Otherwise it is also recommended.
N.B.C. Symphony, conducted by Arturo Toscanini. Two 10" discs, in Set VM–605.

SAINT-SAÉNS, CAMILLE

* *Concerto (Piano and Orchestra) No. 4 in C Minor, Op. 44*
Alfred Cortot and Symphony Orchestra, conducted by Charles Münch. Three 12" discs, in Set VM–367.

* *Carnival of Animals*—an orchestral fantasy
Philadelphia Orchestra, conducted by Leopold Stokowski. Three 12" discs, in Set VM–71.

Danse Macabre
Philadelphia Orchestra, conducted by Leopold Stokowski. 12" disc, No. V–14162.

Samson and Dalila—Opera in 3 acts
Printemps qui commence (Act I) & Mon

coeur s'ouvre a ta voix (Act II). Sigrid
Onegin (contralto, in French) with orchestra. 12″ disc, No. v–7320.

Concerto (Cello and Orchestra) No. 1 in A Minor, Op. 33
Gregor Piatigorsky (cello) and the Chicago
Symphony Orchestra conducted by Freder-
ick Stock. Two 12″ discs (4 sides) in Set
No. cm–x182.

SCHELLING, ERNEST

* *A Victory Ball*—Fantasy for Orchestra
New York Philharmonic-Symphony, conducted by Wilhelm Mengelberg. Two 10″
discs, Nos. v–1127/28.

SCHUBERT, FRANZ

* *Symphony No. 8 in B Minor ("Unfinished")*
London Philharmonic Orchestra, conducted
by Sir Thomas Beecham. Three 12″ discs,
in Set No. cm–330.
Or the equally satisfactory:
Vienna Philharmonic Orchestra, conducted
by Bruno Walter. Three 12″ discs, in Set
v–g9.

OTHER WORKS BY SCHUBERT:

Symphony No. 9, in C Major (1828)
The Chicago Symphony Orchestra, con-

ducted by Frederick Stock. Six 12″ discs,
in Set CM–403.

Piano Quintet in A Major, Op. 114
Artur Schnabel with Mm. Onnou, Prevost
and Mass of the Pro Arte Qt., and Alfred
Hobday. Five 12″ discs, in Set VM–312.

String Quartet No. 8 in B flat, Op. 168
The Busch Quartet. Three 12″ discs, in
Set VM–670.

SCHUMANN, ROBERT

* *Symphony No. 1 in B-flat Major, Op. 38
("Spring")*
Boston Symphony Orchestra, conducted by
Serge Koussevitzky. Four 12″ discs, in Set
VM–655.

OTHER WORKS BY SCHUMANN:

Carnaval
Myra Hess (piano). Three 12″ discs, in
Set VM–476.
Or Glazounov's arrangement for the Ballet
London Philharmonic Orchestra conducted
by Eugene Goossens. Three 12″ discs, in
Set VM–513.

Kinderscenen
Benno Moiseivitch (piano). Two 12″
discs, Nos. V–7705/6.

Piano Quintet in E-flat Major, Op. 44
Artur Schnabel and Pro Arte Quartet.
Four 12″ discs, in Set VM–267.

Recommended Recordings

Concerto (Piano and Orchestra) in A Minor, Op. 54

Myra Hess and Symphony Orchestra, conducted by Walter Goehr. Four 12″ discs, in Set VM-473.

SIBELIUS, JEAN

* *Symphony No. 1 in E Minor, Op. 39*
Symphony Orchestra, conducted by Robert Kajanus. (9 sides) & Karelia—Alla marcia. Five 12″ discs, in Set CM-151.

* *Finlandia—Symphonic Poem*
London Philharmonic Orchestra, conducted by Sir Thomas Beecham. 12″ disc, No. C-69180D.
Or the equally satisfactory:
The Cleveland Orchestra, conducted by Artur Rodzinski. 12″ disc, No. C-11178D.

* *Symphony No. 2 in D Major, Op. 43*
Boston Symphony Orchestra, conducted by Serge Koussevitzky. Six 12″ discs, in Set VM-272.

* *Symphony No. 5 in E-flat Major, Op. 82*
Boston Symphony Orchestra, conducted by Serge Koussevitzky, with Pohjola's Daughter—Symphonic Fantasia, Op. 49. Five 12″ discs, in Set VM-474.

Recommended Recordings

OTHER WORKS BY SIBELIUS:

En Saga—Tone Poem, Op. 9
 Symphony Orchestra, conducted by Eugene
 Goossens, with Valse Triste. Two 12"
 discs, Nos. v-9925/26.

Karelia—Suite for Orchestra, Op. 11
 No. 1—Intermezzo; No. 3—Alla marcia
 (only).
 London Philharmonic Orchestra, conducted
 by Walter Goehr. 12" disc, No. v-12830.
 Alla marcia is also included in album containing the First Symphony.

The Swan of Tuonela—Legend for Orchestra,
Op. 22
 Chicago Symphony Orchestra, conducted by
 Frederick Stock. 12" disc, No. C-11388D.

Pohjola's Daughter—Symphonic Fantasia, Op.
49 (See: Symphony No. 5)

Symphony No. 4 in A Minor, Op. 63
 London Philharmonic Orchestra, conducted
 by Sir Thomas Beecham, in Volume V
 of Sibelius Society with The Return of
 Lemminkäinen, Op. 22, No. 4; The Tempest, Op. 109—Excerpts. Seven 12" discs,
 in Set VM-446. (Also see Tchaikowsky;
 Romeo and Juliet).

SMETANA, FRIEDRICH

* *The Moldau*—Symphonic Poem

With: From Bohemia's Meadows and Forests (No. 4 from "Ma Vlast"). Czech Philharmonic Orchestra, conducted by Rafael
Kubelik. Three 12″ discs, in Set VM–523.

*String Quartet No. 1, in E Minor ("From My
Life")*
Curtis String Quartet. Four 12″ discs, in
Set CM–405.

The Bartered Bride—opera in 3 acts
Complete Opera, sung in Czech, by National Opera Company of Prague. Fifteen
12″ discs, in Set VM–193.
Polka (arr. Orchestra) & Scene of the Co-
medians Minneapolis Symphony Orchestra,
conducted by Eugene Ormandy. 12″ disc,
No. V–8694.

STRAUSS, JOHANN, 1ST.

Radetsky March, Op. 228
Berlin State Opera Orchestra, conducted by
Leo Blech, with J. Strauss, 2nd: Perpetum
mobile. 10″ disc, No. V–4127.

STRAUSS, JOHANN, 2ND.

* *"On the Beautiful Blue Danube"*
Philadelphia Orchestra, conducted by Leo-
pold Stokowski, with Tales from the Vienna
Woods. 12″ disc, No. V–15425.

Album of Strauss Waltzes
Containing: Wine, Women, and Song;

Wiener Blut; Artist's Life; Emperor and Frühlingsstimmen.

Boston "Pops" Orchestra, conducted by Arthur Fiedler. One 10″ and four 12″ discs, in Set VM–445.

Rediscovered Music, from the Paul Löwenberg Collection

Contains: Serial-Tanze; Explosions Polka; Electrofer Polka; Festival Quadrille; Paroxysmen Walzer. The Columbia Broadcasting Symphony, conducted by Howard Barlow. Three 12″ discs, in Set CM–389.

STRAUSS, RICHARD

* *Don Juan*—Symphonic Poem, Op. 20

London Philharmonic Orchestra, conducted by Fritz Busch. Two 12″ discs, in set VM–351.

Or: Less brilliant recording but directed by the composer—

Berlin State Opera Orchestra, conducted by Richard Strauss. Two 12″ imported discs, Nos. D–CA8126/27.

* *Death and Transfiguration*—Symphonic Poem, Op. 24

Philadelphia Orchestra, conducted by Leopold Stokowski. Three 12″ discs, in Set VM–217.

Recommended Recordings

* *Till Eulenspiegel's Merry Pranks*—Symphonic Poem, Op. 28

B.B.C. Symphony Orchestra, conducted by Sir Adrian Boult. Two 12″ discs, Nos. V–11724/25.

OTHER WORKS BY RICHARD STRAUSS:

Also Sprach Zarathustra, Op. 30

Boston Symphony Orchestra, conducted by Serge Koussevitzky. Five 12″ discs, in Set VM–257.

Don Quixote, Op. 35

N. Y. Philharmonic Orchestra, conducted by Sir Thomas Beecham. Five 12″ discs, in Set VM–144.

Strauss' own reading:

Berlin State Opera Orchestra, conducted by Richard Strauss. Five 12″ imported discs, Nos. D–LY6087/91.

Der Rosenkavalier, Op. 59

Selected passages, sung by Lotte Lehmann (Marschallin) ; Elisabeth Schumann (Sophie) ; Maria Olszewska (Oktavian) ; Richard Mayer (Baron Ochs) , and others, with Vienna Philharmonic Orchestra, conducted by Robert Heger. Thirteen 12″ discs, in Set VM–196.

Waltz Movements. Berlin Philharmonic

Orchestra, conducted by Alois Melichar.
12″ imported disc, No. D–CA8268.

Finale Act with Waltzes. E. Ruziczka and
Alexander Kipnis with Orchestra. 12″ disc,
No. V–7894. (Also: Wagner; Meistersinger
—Das schöne Fest, Johannistag).

STRAVINSKY, IGOR

* *The Fire Bird*—Suite for Orchestra
Philadelphia Orchestra, conducted by Leopold Stokowski. Three 12″ discs, in Set
VM–291.

* *Petrouchka*—Suite for Orchestra
Philadelphia Orchestra, conducted by Leopold Stokowski. Four 12″ discs, in Set
VM–574.

* *The Rite of Spring* (Sacre du Printemps)
New York Philharmonic-Symphony, conducted by Igor Stravinsky. Four 12″ discs,
in Set CM–417.

Symphony of Psalms
Vlassof Choir and Symphony Orchestra, conducted by Igor Stravinsky. Three 12″
discs, in Set CM–162.

Capriccio for Piano and Orchestra
Jesús María Sanromá and the Boston Symphony Orchestra, conducted by Serge Koussevitzky. Two 12″ discs, in Set VM–685;
price complete with album.

Recommended Recordings

TAYLOR, DEEMS

* *Through the Looking Glass*—Suite for Orchestra

Columbia Broadcasting Symphony, conducted by Howard Barlow. Four 12″ discs, in Set CM–350.

TCHAIKOWSKY, PETER ILITCH

* *Romeo and Juliet*—Overture-Fantasy

Boston Symphony Orchestra, conducted by Serge Koussevitzky. Three 12″ discs (5 sides) with (Sibelius: Swan White—Maiden with the Roses). VM–347.

* *Concerto (Piano and Orchestra) No. 1 in B-flat Minor, Op. 23*

Arthur Rubinstein and London Symphony Orchestra, conducted by John Barbirolli. Four 12″ discs in Set VM–180.

Second Choice: Egon Petri and London Philharmonic Orchestra, conducted by Walter Goehr. Four 12″ discs in Set CM–318.

* *Symphony No. 4 in F Minor, Op. 36*

Boston Symphony Orchestra, conducted by Serge Koussevitzky. Five 12″ discs (9 sides) with String Serenade, Op. 48—Valse (1 side), in Set VM–327.

* *1812: Ouverture Solenelle, Op. 49*

Boston "Pops" Orchestra, conducted by Ar-

Recommended Recordings

thur Fiedler. Two 12″ discs (4 sides) in
Set VM–515.

* *Symphony No. 5 in E Minor, Op. 64*
The Cleveland Orchestra, conducted by Artur Rodzinski. Five 12″ discs (10 sides) in
Set CM–406.

* *Nutcracker Suite, Op. 71–a*
London Philharmonic Orchestra, conducted
by Eugene Goossens. Three 12″ discs (6
sides) in Set V–G5.
Also suggested:
Swan Lake Ballet—Excerpts, Op. 20. London Philharmonic Orchestra, conducted by
Antal Dorati. Four 12″ discs (8 sides) in
Set CM–349.

* *Symphony No. 6 in B Minor, Op. 74 ("Pathetique")*
Boston Symphony Orchestra, conducted by
Serge Koussevitzky. Five 12″ discs (10
sides) in Set VM–85.
Also recommended as the finest though
Victor has but recently issued it for American music lovers.
Berlin Philharmonic Orchestra, conducted
by Wilhelm Furtwängler. Six 12″ discs (12
sides), in Set VM–553.

Trio for piano, violin and 'cello, Op. 50
Yehudi Menuhin, Maurice Eisenberg,
Hephzibah Menuhin. Six 12″ discs (11
sides, last blank) in Set VM–388.

Recommended Recordings

Eugene Onegin—Opera in 3 acts, Op. 24
Suggested excerpts:
Lenski's Aria (Act II) "Faint echo of youth"
& (Borodin: Prince Igor—Vladimir's Aria).
Charles Kullman (tenor, in German) with
Orchestra. 12″ disc, No. C–9099M.
Waltz (Act II) & Polonaise (Act III).
Royal Opera Orchestra (Stockholm), con-
ducted by Armas Järnefelt. 12″ disc, No.
D–25325.

The Queen of Spades, Opera in 3 acts, Op. 68
O viens mon doux berger, (Act II). Emmy
Destinn and Maria Duchene (in French).
12″ imported disc, No. G–DK105.

WAGNER, RICHARD

* *Overture to "The Flying Dutchman"*
London Philharmonic Orchestra, conducted
by Sir Thomas Beecham. Two 12″ discs,
in Set CM–X107. (Also—Tannhäuser—
Einzug der Gäste).

* *Overture to "Tannhäuser"*
Overture and Venusberg Music (Paris Version) and Prelude to Act III (arr. Stokowski). The Philadelphia Orchestra, conducted by Leopold Stokowski. Five 12″
discs, in Set VM–530.
Overture (Only).
London Philharmonic Orchestra, conducted

Recommended Recordings

by Sir Thomas Beecham. Two 12″ discs, in
Set CM–X123. (Also—Borodin: Prince Igor
—Polovtsi March).

* *"Prelude and Love-Death" from "Tristan
and Isolde"*
Berlin Philharmonic Orchestra, conducted
by Wilhelm Furtwängler. Two 12″ imported discs, Nos. D–CA8099 & CA8156.

* *Prelude to "Die Meistersinger"*
An album containing: Meistersinger Prelude; Götterdämmerung—Rhine Journey
and Funeral March; Parsifal—Prelude to
Act I. Berlin State Opera Orchestra, conducted by Karl Muck. Five 12″ discs, in Set
VM–67.

* *Siegfried Idyll*
Vienna Philharmonic Orchestra, conducted
by Bruno Walter. Two 12″ discs, in Set
V–G12.

* *Magic Fire Music from "Die Walküre"*
The Philadelphia Orchestra, conducted by
Leopold Stokowski. 12″ disc, No. V–15800.

* *"Forest Murmurs" from "Siegfried"*
(See next item)

* *"Good Friday Spell" from "Parsifal"*
Alexander Kipnis (bs); Fritz Wolff (T)
with Bayreuth Festival Orchestra, conducted
by Siegfried Wagner. Two 12″ discs, Nos.
C–67370/71D. (Also—Siegfried—Forest Murmurs)

Recommended Recordings

Das Rheingold—Excerpts (arr. Stokowski)
Philadelphia Orchestra, conducted by Leopold Stokowski. Three 12″ discs, in Set VM–179.

Ziegfried
Nothung! Nothung! (Forging Song), Act I.
Lauritz Melchior and the Philadelphia Orchestra, conducted by Eugene Ormandy.
(Also—Walküre—Wintersturme). 10″ disc,
No. V–2035.

Finale Act III—Duet Brünnhilde and Siegfried—Heil dir, Sonne! Florence Easton
(S) and Lauritz Melchior (T), with London Symphony, conducted by Robert Heger.
Four 12″ discs, in Set V–167. (Also includes
Prelude to Act I.)

Götterdämmerung
Immolation Scene, Act III
Frida Leider and the Berlin State Opera
Orchestra, conducted by Leo Blech. Two
12″ imported discs, Nos. G–D2025/26.

From Victor's Three Famous Scenes (Wagner) there is a less satisfactory version by
the reigning Wagnerian favorite. Götterdämmerung—Immolation Scene (Flagstad);
Tristan und Isolde—Love Duet, Act II
(Flagstad and Melchior); Leibestod, Act
III. (Flagstad), with San Francisco Opera

Orchestra, conducted by Edwin McArthur.
Five 12″ discs, in Set VM–644.

WEBER, CARL MARIA VON

* *Invitation to the Dance,* Op. 65 (orch.
Berlioz)
B.B.C. Symphony Orchestra, conducted by
Arturo Toscanini. 12″ disc, No. V–15192.
* *Overture to "Der Freischutz"*
London Philharmonic Orchestra, conducted
by Sir Thomas Beecham. 12″ disc, No.
C–68986D.
* *Overture to "Oberon"*
The London Philharmonic Orchestra, con-
ducted by Sir Thomas Beecham. 12″ disc,
No. C–69410D.

Suggested Reading

BACH—by C. F. Abdy William (*Dent & Sons, London*)

BEETHOVEN—by Harvey Grace (*Kegan, Paul, Trench, Trubner & Co., London*)

BEETHOVEN, His Spiritual Development—by J. W. N. Sullivan (*A. A. Knopf*)

BERLIOZ—by J. H. Elliot (*E. P. Dutton & Co.*)

THE UNKNOWN BRAHMS—by R. H. Schauffer (*Dodd, Mead & Co.*)

CHOPIN, His Life—by William Murdoch (*John Murray, London*)

DEBUSSY, Man and Artist—by Oscar Thompson (*Dodd, Mead & Co.*)

ANTONIN DVOŘÁK—by Karel Hoffmeister (*John Lane, London*)

CESAR FRANCK—from the French of Vincent D'Indy (*John Lane, London*)

Suggested Reading

EDVARD GRIEG—by David Monrad—Johansen (*Princeton Univ. Press*)

HANDEL—by Romain Rolland (*H. Holt & Co.*)

MENDELSSOHN, a Second Elijah—by Schima Kaufman (*T. Y. Crowell Co.*)

MOUSSORGSKY—by Oscar von Riesemann (*A. A. Knopf*)

MOZART—by Marcia Davenport (*Grosset & Dunlap*)

RACHMANINOFF'S RECOLLECTIONS—by Oscar von Riesemann (*Macmillan*)

MY MUSICAL LIFE—by N. Rimsky-Korsakoff (*A. A. Knopf*)

ROSSINI, a Study in Tragi-Comedy—by Francis Toye (*W. Heinemann, London*)

SCHUBERT, the Man and His Circle—by Newman Flower (*F. A. Stokes Co.*)

SCHUMANN, a Life of Suffering—by Victor Basch (*A. A. Knopf*)

SIBELIUS—by Cecil Gray (*Oxford Univ. Press*)

JOHANN STRAUSS, Father and Son—by H. E. Jacob (*Greystone Press*)

STRAVINSKY, an Autobiography (*Simon & Schuster*)

Suggested Reading

RICHARD STRAUSS, the Man and His Work— by H. T. Finck (*Little, Brown & Co.*)

BELOVED FRIEND, the Story of Tchaikowsky— by Bowen & von Meck (*Random House*)

WAGNER, as Man and Artist—by Ernest Newman (*A. A. Knopf*)

———

How MUSIC GREW, from Prehistoric Times to the Present Day—by Marion Bauer & E. R. Peyser (*E. P. Dutton*)

THE HISTORY OF MUSIC—by Cecil Gray (*A. A. Knopf*)

A SURVEY OF CONTEMPORARY MUSIC—by Cecil Gray (*Oxford Univ. Press*)

THE INTERNATIONAL CYCLOPEDIA OF MUSIC AND MUSICIANS—edited by Oscar Thompson (*Dodd, Mead & Co.*) Especially recommended. It is readable, intelligent, and dependable.

Index

Index

[299]

Index